Win an Election

A Complete Guide for
Winning at the Polls

I0412789

By Robert Chartuk

A Real Life Series book

Published in the United States of America

ISBN-13: 978-1499338102

To receive free information and helpful tips and updates about running for office, visit us at:

www.WinAnElection.org

DEDICATION

To anyone who's sweated it out on election night.

TABLE OF CONTENTS

FIGHT BACK

Government is happening all around us and the reaction of most people is either anger or apathy. They're mad because they're overtaxed and overregulated by politicians living off their hard-earned dollars. Or they just bury their heads in the sand and let someone else call the shots—and keep paying and paying.

Come on folks, get in the game! Nothing's going to change unless people like you step up to the plate and do what it takes to win. If you knew you had a fighting chance, would you be willing to run?

Here's a Real Life Series guide showing you exactly what you need to do to take back your government. From developing yourself as a candidate and assembling a campaign team to raising money and devising a winning plan of attack, all the ammunition you need to win is at your fingertips. Don't wait to get started—The people are counting on you!

INTRODUCTION

The folks here at Real Life wouldn't put you through something we haven't gone through. We've run numerous elections and were even on the ballot a few times ourselves. We're Summa Cum Laude graduates of the School of Hard Campaign Knocks and we're sure if you follow our lead, your chances of winning will soar.

As you read, don't worry about absorbing everything all at once. We give you an overview of a winning campaign plan in Chapter Thirteen and a Checklist to make sure you cover all the bases.

Plus, at the end of each chapter, you can eavesdrop on the campaign of Mary Morgan, candidate for the Centerville Town Council who suffers the slings and arrows of a tough election, and experience her exciting conclusion.

We also include definitions of political terms so you can ace the lingo (words marked with an asterisk are defined in the Glossary).

From building your narrative and raising money to getting the nod and managing your campaign, here's everything you'll need to win.

Are You Crazy?

You're an upstanding citizen, member of the civic association, Rotary Club volunteer, and spokesperson for your community in the fight against a monstrous mega mall they want to build near your home. Or maybe you're just a taxpayer who's mad as hell and aren't going to take it anymore.

The phone rings and it's your neighbor asking if you're interested in running for the town council to throw out the politicians who support the mega mall. Visions of filibusters have always danced in your head and you know you can do a better job than the bozos currently in office, so you say, "What the heck, I'll give it a go and maybe make a difference."

Plus, in the back of your mind you're thinking elected office might help your business prospects or change people's lives for the better or maybe get that shiftless brother-in-law of yours a job or...but first you have to check with the spouse.

"Running for office! Are you crazy? You're out too many nights as it is. How much will this cost? Who would ever vote for you?"

"Don't worry honey, I can do this. Plus, it will be fun."

"Okay, but don't expect any help from me." (Famous last words from a significant other, as you will soon find out.)

You smile that politician's smile, but deep inside, your brain is screaming: *What do I do now?*

Congratulations. You've just been bitten by the Election Bug,* and don't count on breaking its grip any time soon. A frightening prospect, yes, but the rewards can be substantial.

Thankfully, we're here to make you a winner. So take a deep breath, read carefully, and enjoy the ride!

CHAPTER ONE
THE MAKING OF A
GOOD CANDIDATE

"Everyone wants to be Cary Grant. Even I want to be Cary Grant."—Cary Grant.

First, Some Introspection: Aside from your good looks and burning desire to make a difference, why should people vote for you? What do you have to offer? How's your mien? Do you have gravitas? (Two fancy words for Do you have what it takes?) If you were to describe yourself in a couple of paragraphs, what would you say? This, in fact, is your story—your narrative, resume, record—what you will present to the voters to win their support.

Real Life Scenario: Civil rights lawyer Bella Abzug, a hat-wearing powder keg with a funny name, was said to be "born yelling." She was beloved by her New York City constituency* because she was one of them and was elected to Congress three times. The voters may not have loved her on all of the issues, they just loved her.

Let's describe an ideal candidate (for illustration purposes only—don't be discouraged if you're not all this just yet):

Mary Morgan is an active member of her community; she's involved with the Rotary Club and the Friends of the Library and has operated a financial services business on Main Street for 25 years. She attends town council meetings and gets quoted in the paper when she speaks up on local issues. She's active in charitable work and knows a lot of people. She takes care of herself and dresses well. She's a good listener and can take advice. Her family, friends and neighbors think highly of her and would be willing to help in an election campaign. She comes off as confident and competent and leaves a positive image in people's minds. When it's mentioned that she's running for office they think, "Yeah, I'd vote for her."

So what if you're not Mary? You can write your own story, maybe even a better one. Start with the office you want to pursue. If it's the town council, attend their meetings. Get educated on what their responsibilities are and how they operate. Pay attention to what they're up to and speak up on a few matters. Follow them in the media; Google them. Go to their websites and Social Media pages (if they don't have them, you'll already have a leg up when you go digital). Seek out people in the know—they'll be happy to fill you in. If your main motivator is stopping the mega mall proposed for your neighborhood, go to every meeting on the subject or organize a few of your own to show off your leadership skills.

Real Life Scenario: Caesar Trunzo, the late state senator from New York, went to everything. He showed up at historical society meetings, Lion's Club breakfasts, hearings to discuss developments like the mega mall. If your son became an Eagle Scout, he went to the dinner and gave the kid a proclamation. Everyone knew him and he basked in the attention. When Election Day rolled around, he was a shoo-in because no matter who you were or what you did, he took an interest and made an impression.

Speak to the people you see at public meetings and find out why they're there. Get to know their issues and concerns and see how the elected officials are handling them. They may be getting ignored, mistreated, or blown off. You could be their savior and they would support you, so get nosy and bore in.

Join local organizations and get involved. Volunteer for something; show up. Meet people; see if you resonate with them. Politics is a people business and the more people you know (and know who you are), the better your chances of getting ahead. Maybe you don't run a local business, but you are dedicated and skillful where you work and know what it takes to follow a budget and make ends meet. You have friends and are a devoted parent. You attend school events and are on the PTA. You've joined the Lions Club and are a member of a union. The point is, with a little effort, you can constantly build up your narrative and make yourself relevant and compelling to a lot of people.

> **Bonus:** Military veterans, with their training, expertise, and patriotism, (not to mention how great they look in uniform), make excellent political candidates.

Why Are You Running?

Answer the question in front of a mirror; explain it to your spouse or close friends—if you can't give a compelling, sincere, believable reason in two or three sentences, then you better figure it out ASAP or you'll be in big trouble out on the campaign trail. After you're comfortable with your "Elevator Speech"—a brief statement that sums up your intentions in the 30 seconds or so it would take for an elevator ride—practice it until you can do it in your sleep.

Your Platform: As you solidify your narrative and start figuring out what's on the minds of the voters, you can build your platform. This is a brief 1-2 page statement on who you are, why you are running and where you stand on the issues. It must tell the electorate* what you are going to do for them and make a compelling case on why they should vote for you. If you're against the mega mall, make it part of your platform. But maybe your area needs the jobs the mall would bring, so your platform should have an economic component. People may be worried about taxes and out-of-control government spending—What's your position on that?

> **Real Life Scenario:** When he ran for president, U.S. Senator Ted Kennedy was asked in a CBS News interview: "Why do you want to be president?" He had no answer. His stunned silence and fumbling response probably cost him the Democratic nomination which went to the incumbent,* Jimmy Carter (who then lost to Ronald Reagan, a former actor if that tells you anything).

In building your platform, be wary of a couple of things:

- **You can't stand for everything.**
- **You can't stand for everything your opponents stand for.**
- **For everything you stand for, someone else stands for the opposite.**
- **You can't be everything to everyone** (though we've seen some politicians* try).

Would you consider yourself a Conservative or a Liberal, Republican or Democrat? Do you think taxes are too high or should people pay more because government needs to provide more services? How do you feel about the mega mall? Do you think it should be blocked to protect the environment or is it needed to create jobs? After you figure out who you are and what you stand for, stay true to your values and go out and impress enough people to win.

Out of the Blue: Once you've made up your mind and have your act together to run, you may find that serendipity, timing, or sheer luck puts you at the right place at the right time. Despite not having run for office before, you can easily come out of the blue to win the hearts of voters. People love it when someone stands up for no other reason than to shake up the system and give the status quo a run for its money. Many candidates are groomed and re-invented by their parties to win a particular seat. But there are many still who, by the sheer force of character, preparation, and good timing, take the election by storm.

Ride In On An Issue: Another way to win an election is to take advantage of an unprecedented event. New York's Carolyn McCarthy lived her life as a mother and nurse as she carried out a peaceful existence in suburbia. Running for office was about the last thing on her mind when a deranged gunman killed her husband and seriously wounded her son aboard a Long Island Rail Road commuter train. Instantly, she became an anti-gun celebrity and in less than a year, defeated an entrenched pro-gun incumbent for a seat in the U.S. Congress.

Real Life Scenario: Although he didn't become president, a complete unknown named Ross Perot dropped in from outer space in 1992 to win a huge amount of votes and spur a national movement when he parlayed his goofy straight-talk about our nation's finances into a serious bid* for the White House.

Whether you are fighting a mega mall in your neighborhood or advocating a ban on automatic weapons, your single issue can very well strike a chord with the electorate and overnight, set the stage for a winning campaign. Talk to people, find out what's on their minds, and stay alert. There are always issues out there that can propel you to victory.

Attitude: Serving in an elected office is an honor and a privilege. People are putting their trust in you and the last thing you want to project is a holier than thou attitude. Be humble. Be sincere and always remember that the people you look

Real Life Scenario: Colorado Senator Gary Hart was the frontrunner* for the Democratic nomination for president in 1987 when he said to reporters asking about rumors of extra-marital affairs: "Follow me around. I don't care. If anybody wants to put a tail on me, go ahead. They'll be very bored." They took him up on his offer and he promptly led them to the yacht, "Monkey Business," where he was photographed with his girlfriend. That was the end of his campaign.

down on or take for granted can vote you out in a heartbeat. While it may be expeditious to cow tow to the political bosses, wealthy donors and insiders that help get you there, it's the lowly voter that will put you back to where you belong.

Arrogance: Nothing turns people off faster than an arrogant politician. Some long-serving officials think they're rock stars as they control millions in taxpayer dollars and have people bowing at their feet. Remember, you'll see the same people climbing up the ladder as you will falling back down, so don't let it go to your head.

> **Beware:**
> **Man vs. Woman**

Men must be careful not to come across as bullying or chauvinistic toward women. A spirited tone acceptable in an argument with a man could be inappropriate against a woman. Mistreatment of an opponent will give their supporters extra motivation to beat you.

Real Life Scenario: When Rick Lazio debated Hillary Clinton during their U.S. Senate race, he strode across the stage with a "Freedom From Soft Money" pledge and demanded she sign it. She refused. The maneuver was a flop. Not only did he invade her space, she dismissed his challenge making him look like a loser. His stunt was panned by the media and cost him many female votes.

Scrutiny: Your opponents will look for every angle to diminish you in the eyes of the voters. Have you been voting? Have you paid your taxes? Have you always been a member of your particular party or did you just switch over to run for office? How long have you lived in the area? Are you a Carpet Bagger?* Go over the details of your life. If there's anything you need to fix, fix it. If there's anything you have to explain, be prepared to explain it.

Are there any skeletons in your closet? Expect that anything you've ever done will be dredged up and used against you. If there are show stoppers out there like a murder rap or you have two wives, discuss them with your campaign team before they come up. The best bet is to be honest and don't try to hide anything. Heck, Bill Clinton confessed to smoking marijuana and got to be president (though he didn't inhale).

Real Life Scenario: Meg Whitman, who was president of Hewlett Packard and eBay and worth millions, ran for governor of California with one little handicap: she didn't vote in any election until she was 46 years old. Her opponents had a field day with her lack of participation in the electoral process and she lost, badly.

Real Life Scenario: When New York Governor Elliot Spitzer was forced to resign after a prostitution scandal, his lieutenant, David Paterson, inherited the job and was immediately put under the microscope. Rather than have the media drag the skeletons out of his closet day after day, he held a press conference to get it all out in one fell swoop and admitted to a laundry list of past indiscretions from drug use to cheating on his wife. Paterson was able to limit the negative coverage to just a blip on the radar screen, but he was such a train wreck he had no chance of getting the Democratic nod* and declined to run for his own term.

Mary took stock in her situation and thought to herself: *You know what? I can do this! I've been to enough town meetings and I understand what's going on. They're spending way too much taxpayer money and I don't think they're managing things very well. With my business experience and head for numbers, I can make a difference. Plus, I know a lot of people through Rotary and the library and they're pretty unhappy about taxes and town hall. I think they'll respond well to someone who'll fight taxes. I've spoken out against the mega mall and I've participated in all of the clean-ups along Mott's River, so I think I have a pretty good environmental record. I can win!*

She made up her mind to run and told her husband, Tom.

"Are you nuts," he said with that funny look on his face. "With your business and clubs, where will you find the time?"

Mary expected his reaction. "But honey, this is something I've thought about for a long time. I know what's going on in our town and I can do a good job. Let's give it a try."

"Okay, but don't expect too much help from me."

Excited, Mary took to the phone to break the news to her friends and they were excited too. She thought about a campaign team, making note of people from her clubs and associates who might help. No turning back now.

Mary practiced in the mirror:

I've lived in Centerville my entire life, raised a family here and run my own business. I'm tired of seeing our young people—who we pay dearly to educate—leave because they can't find jobs and I hate to see our senior citizens struggle because they can't afford the taxes. Ladies and gentlemen, people are voting with their feet. They are packing up and leaving and do you know what happened last year in Centerville for the first time in history? We actually lost population! After a century of steady growth, our area is in decline and the reason is high taxes and job loss. Our town council's answer to that? Instead of sharpening their pencils and finding ways to cut spending, they gave us another tax increase. I'm running for the Centerville Town Council because I want to reverse this awful trend and have the government work for us, not the other way around. I want people to be able to afford to live here, not work day after day just to pay taxes. If you join me, I know we can do it. Are you with me?

CHAPTER TWO

YOU AS THE CANDIDATE

2

How do you feel? How do you look? Do you have a style nobody has the guts to tell you is hopelessly out of date? As intelligent and caring and wonderful you may be on the inside, voters are still going to judge the book by its cover. Regardless of your brilliant dissertations on the stump, if your clothes are wrinkled and you have a tie wider than a 747, people are not going to take you seriously. Attracting followers is much easier if you carry yourself like a winner.

You only get one chance to make a first impression, so make sure you look good. Gentlemen, buy a couple of new suits, shirts, and appropriate ties. Ask your haberdasher, he'll know. Avoid ties in the shape of a fish or other weird designs. Wear a little flag or your Marine Corps pin if you were one—something small and unobtrusive that people will notice if they share the affiliation. Otherwise, don't come in with a "Hi, I'm oblivious" display. Avoid hats, unless that's been your style and they look good on you. If you appear before the Lion's Club and they give you a hat, it's okay to put it on for the moment, but don't wear it to the Elks. If you're going on TV, have the studio powder you up so you don't have that glossy, sweaty look.

Real Life Scenario: In his face off against John F. Kennedy—the nation's first ever televised debate—Richard Nixon appeared clammy and sickly vs. Kennedy's calm and confident. From that point on, Nixon's campaign for president was doomed.

Campaign clothing for women is a little more complicated and no question about it, you have a tougher job than men when it comes to attire. People will judge your appearance more harshly, so keep it middle of the road—too flashy and you'll turn people off—and not too much jewelry and definitely not too much perfume.

Act Like a Pro: Inexperienced candidates often send signals that undermine their credibility. Since people make decisions based on subtle cues and signals, political consultant Ron Nehring offers these tips to elevate your aura from amateur to pro:

- ➤ **Flag Ties:** Ronald Reagan was a great American patriot, and he didn't have to prove it by wearing a flag tie—a novelty you should probably put on eBay. Want to show your patriotism? Wear a small flag pin on your lapel.

- ➤ **Cheap-o Pens:** "Ok, let me write your number down," and while you're writing, the person is looking at your hand. If it's holding a Bic pen with the end chewed off, you don't look very impressive. Mont Blanc gets $450 for a pen not because it doesn't matter, but because it does. Yours doesn't have to break the bank, but a proper pen sends a subtle signal that you have your act together.

- ➤ **Free Offer! Business Cards:** Companies like Vista Print offer "free!" business cards using generic templates with their logo on the back (free for you is free advertising for them). If you order these, while you're at it, have them add "I'm not taking this race seriously enough to invest in sending the right message to donors, volunteers, and stakeholders"* on the back.

Spending a few bucks on the right cards shows you mean business.

- ➤ **"I Lost Weight" Shirts:** So you dropped 20 pounds walking all those neighborhoods–fantastic! But if you don't trade in your old shirts for ones that fit your new neck size, you're going to look like an addict, and your sloppy appearance will show in all those Facebook photos.

- ➤ **Clinton-Era Shoes:** Look down right now. If your shoes weren't purchased during the Obama Administration, take them off, put them in the closet, and wear them for gardening. When you're at events, it's surprising how often people are looking down. High-end Hugo Boss shoes aren't required, but yours should be new and clean.

- ➤ **Dark Button-Down Shirts:** If you're wearing a black button-down shirt, a tie and a blazer, congratulations, you look like a bouncer at a bar. Ditch the Sopranos look and go with a white or light blue shirt. Still have doubts? Turn on C-SPAN. See any elected officials with your bouncer costume?

- ➤ **Rookie@gmail.com:** That's the message you're sending with your "I'm using this email address until I lose" Gmail or Yahoo account. For $10 at Go-Daddy.com you can register your own private domain name, then have email to that address forwarded to your regular account. Mary@MorganForCouncil.com looks a lot better than Mary!1965@yahoo.com.

- ➤ **Loner=Loser:** Showing up at the chamber of commerce lunch by yourself tells everyone you have no supporters. Instead, arrive with an assistant whose job it is to take names and numbers for follow up. When you're working the crowd and are confronted with someone who wants to chew your ear off, make sure your wing man leads you away so you have time to connect with everyone else.

> **Bonus:** Let a member of the group you're meeting with know when you're coming, and have them meet you in the parking lot. Walk in together to show other members you have supporters already on board.

Real Life Scenario: We know a surfer who regularly faces down large waves that could easily kill him. He's into politics and when he walks into a room, he knows there won't be too many people who have the guts to do what he does. Needless to say, he has a built-in mien and the gravitas to impress people and not be intimidated by blowhards.

Confidence: For any situation, go in with positive thoughts. You know you've studied the issues and have people behind you. You've done your homework. You're convinced you have the dedication, knowledge, energy and skill to be a great leader. This will give you huge confidence and make you a better person—and a better candidate—than those you are running against. Never be intimidated. You've put in the time and effort to make yourself knowledgeable and relevant and never once should you believe you're not as good as the other guy (if they've been in office for a while, it's almost a guarantee they're weasels and you are better than them).

Public Speaking: How you come across when you speak is a critical factor not only in elections, but many aspects of life. And it's not just what you say, but how you say it that's important. As a candidate, the good news is you don't have to reinvent the wheel every time you speak. Your key points won't change very much and once you nail them down you should have no problem orating like a pro.

Let's go over a few tips that will make you a better speaker almost immediately and help tame the butterflies every single one of us gets when standing before a crowd.

Preparation: Knowing what you're going to say and how you're going to say it is your best defense against blowing it. Since public speaking is such a vital part of campaigning make sure you devote the time and energy to get it right. Pore over your narrative and your platform and figure out exactly what you want to say. Think about what you believe in and what moves you. Write it out in long hand and make edits. Go over it with others and polish until you're proud. You can stand up and recite the Pledge of Allegiance because you know it well— Do the same with your speech.

> **Real Life Scenario:** "According to most studies, people's number one fear is public speaking. Number two is death. Now this means, to the average person, if you have to go to a funeral, you're better off in the casket than doing the eulogy."—Jerry Seinfeld

Practice: Once you have a script you believe in, let it rip. Video yourself or practice in front of a mirror. Deliver it to family and friends. Do it in your sleep. Get to the point where you could belt it out in front of a firing squad. It's not like you are reciting verses from a text book—this is you, your story, your words—so you shouldn't need to work off notes or a teleprompter.

Your Moment: Once you hit the stage, this is your moment—all eyes are on you. Show off, be proud. People will appreciate you being there and will even clap. Soak it up. Be a ham and the more you do it, the more you'll like it and the better you'll get.

Personality: Your presentation is not just words, it's you! Put your personality into it, use your own words and phrases. Move around, make gestures, and animate your face. Just like an actor, you can convey your message with body language and facial expressions.

Uhs and Duhs, You Know and Other Annoying Phrases: Disrupting your speech with uhs and duhs means one thing: You're not comfortable with your presentation because you haven't practiced it enough. Nobody sings, "Happy birthday, umm, to you." If your train of thought is derailed by ahs and you knows, keep practicing until you get it right.

Eye Contact: A key element of interpersonal communication (fancy word we learned in college) is eye contact. It's actually much easier to maintain eye contact with a group than a single individual since you can keep your eyes moving and not have to lock onto a single person. Look to the people in the front and the back and the sides while making your points and if you see anyone who's really responsive, speak directly to them from time to time so the crowd thinks you're old friends.

Speaking one-on-one is a little more challenging. You don't want to stare them down or fixate on their mole, so look away when necessary so neither of you feel uncomfortable.

Humor: Telling a joke or funny story is a

Real Life Scenario: A candidate at a civic forum was much younger than his opponents and a quick observation helped him make light of the fact. There was a group of cub scouts in the audience and the candidate opened his remarks with: "Thanks to the cub scouts here tonight, I'm not the youngest person in the room." He then made a point about the importance of community involvement at an early age and showed more energy and enthusiasm than his older opponents.

great way to break the ice and win over a crowd. If you open your presentation with a funny quip or observation, people will be more inclined to pay attention and come away with a positive feeling. They may not be able to recall what your speech was about, but they'll remember you.

Whenever possible, get out from behind the lectern and interact with your audience. Nothing's more boring than someone sitting up there speaking down at the crowd. Move over a few steps and address the people to the left and then to the right; move forward and appeal to the center—don't stand there with your feet planted in concrete. Be animated and energetic, but don't overdo it. Vary your facial expressions, smile a lot; act like you're interested in what you're saying.

The Diamonds: Public speaker extraordinaire and professional sales trainer Floyd Wickman breaks down a great speech into the four facets of a diamond. Incorporate these techniques into your presentation and you will have your audiences eating out of your hand:

1 **Audience Participation:** Raise your hand if you've ever been to an event where the speaker was glued behind a podium and never interacted with the crowd. Pretty boring, huh? And did you remember anything? Get your audience to participate. It's hard for people to doze off when you're constantly asking them questions. "Show of hands—Who's tired of paying high taxes?" Get them to agree with what you're saying; make your speech a two-way street. Who's with me on that?

Bonus: Use people's names. Make sure you have some familiar faces in the crowd and pose some of your questions to them: "Bill, have you ever heard of that before?" By referring to a few people personally, the audience will think you know everybody.

2 **Stories:** Practically every point you make—especially about yourself and what you offer the voters—can be presented through a story. Don't just say you were from Dubuque, talk about what it was like growing up among the corn fields of Iowa and how Mrs. Jones next door taught you the value of respecting others. Be poignant and entertaining.

Real Life Scenario: One candidate nailed home the high cost of living when he told a story about senior citizens forced back into the work place. "Standing in Velcro sneakers all day greeting people at Walmart is not what they expected for their golden years," he told his audience.

Tell them about a family that had to move because they couldn't afford the taxes and let them know how you will make things more affordable. Offer a vignette from the campaign trail and how you enjoyed hearing about the Girl Scout food drive. People will listen to real life stories a lot more intently than a recitation of your resume.

3 **Visuals:** A picture is worth...a thousand dollars, according to Wickman, who asks his students, "Why tell someone when you can show them? If you're meeting with a potential donor, show them your winning game plan. Show the mall opponents the traffic statistics. Use the census chart, pictures, graphs, dollar bills. While words may be a politico's* stock in trade, visuals get people's attention and hold it. Use them as another weapon in your campaign arsenal.

> **Bonus:** Show Your Stuff—Power Point slides, flip charts, audio/video clips, voluminous reports, something from your pocket, are but a few ways to employ your visuals.

4 **Take Action:** At the end of your presentation, ask your audience to take action: vote for you, give a donation, volunteer. Come right out and say it; make The Ask. Who's with me on that?

Make it clear what their action will mean:

- "Your vote will mean less taxes and reduced government spending—can I count on you to help make our area more affordable?"
- "A small donation, the price of a couple of cups of coffee, will go a long way toward helping us stop the mega mall. Is that something you're willing to do?"
- "Just a few hours of your time will send a message to town hall that we just can't afford politics as usual. Are

you available during the day or would evenings be better?"

Diamond from Floyd Wickman: "Be yourself in your presentations, let your personality come through. Be animated, smile, laugh, have some fun. Even if you're nervous or unsure, overlay the four facets on everything you do and people will see you as a seasoned pro."

CAMPAIGN UPDATE

Mary came downstairs and Tom almost fell off his chair. She had been shopping and was showing off one of her new outfits. She looked professional and smart. She had new shoes, smart jewelry and a small American flag pin on her lapel.

"Are you running for the town council or president?" her husband asked, duly impressed.

Mary's confidence shot up from the feedback.

"My card," she said handing him a glossy that included her email address:

Mary@MorganForCouncil.com

"Wow! Will you have time for dinner, Madam Councilwoman?"

"No. I had a light snack and don't want to be sleepy during my meeting. Plus, I'm watching my weight, but thank you for asking. I really appreciate your support."

"You sound like a politician already."

CHAPTER THREE
MONEY

⟶

$$$ "There are two things that are important in politics. The first is money, and I can't remember what the second one is."—19th Century political boss Mark Hanna$$

Now that we've gotten that out of the way, let's talk about the prime motivator for campaigns and elections: money. Whether it's a $100,000 library budget, $10 million bond act, or billion dollar spending plan, elected officials get to make decisions on huge amounts of other people's money. In fact, your congressional rep. will vote on budgets measured in the trillions–ungodly sums that impact almost every aspect of our lives.

And with money comes power: Depending on your position, you can have a fancy office with a big staff, get your brother-in-law a patronage* job, award a consulting contract to a contributor, or route a highway through someone's back yard. Whether it's a decision on education, immigration, building a pipeline, or starting a war, politicians make decisions that affect people in more ways than you can imagine.

Real Life Scenario: Every summer, the dynamic duo of Bill and Hillary Clinton spend time in the Hamptons, tapping the glitterati–movie stars, magnates, philanthropists–for all they're worth. With war chests reaching into the millions, the Clintons know money means victory. Where will you get yours?

It's true, some people go into public service with visions of grandeur—stopping the mega mall, cutting taxes, or just doing the right thing for their fellow man. But most of the time, the major motivator is money and power and once people get a piece of it, they'll do anything to keep it.

> **Real Life Scenario:** "You know what kind of person it takes to run for President? Not normal. They could start out okay, but by the time they reach that level they've sold their soul to the devil so many times and stomped the guts out of enough people that they are definitely not like you and me, not even close."—David Baldacci

Beware: Politics

For every benevolent soul, there's a pack of wolves out there working a lot harder than you to milk the system for all its worth. So to survive, even the most true-blue office seeker must participate in the rough and tumble of politics.

Money sources for your race will emerge at every turn, or be shut down, depending on how you play your cards. In the next chapter, we will detail how you can tap into these pots of gold, so for now, we'll just cover the basics.

Self-Funding: If you can't kick in a few bucks of your own into the coffer, how can you ask others to make a commitment to your cause? Likewise, if you can't generate some seed money, maybe you're not exactly in a good position to run for office.

Family Plan: Start with yourself, family, friends, neighbors, and associates. Again, if you can't convince them to chip in, maybe your dream of being elected—or your political skills—aren't as viable as you think.

Your Cause: Are you campaigning against the mega mall? If so, people will back you for opposing the monstrosity. Maybe you are pro-union, anti-gun, or a member of the Green movement—where you come from is where your funds will come from. People will support those who support their issues. All you have to do is ask.

Your ability to raise money will be directly linked to your campaign platform. You can ask those who recruited you to the mega mall battle to take up a collection. Or you can organize a Stop the Mega Mall Rally yourself and pass the hat (and sign up campaign volunteers while you're at it). On the other hand, maybe you support the mall and there's a whole host of union workers, trade associations, and even the developers themselves looking to sweep you in. For every cause, there's a group behind it and if you espouse their views, they will open their pocketbooks. Later, we will cover what it means to accept this kind of money.

Your Party: Republican, Democrat, Conservative, Liberal, Working Families, Green—A candidate can run under various banners and these organizations can be a key source of funds. The major parties have the wherewithal to handle most aspects of your campaign, including paying for it. As a party candidate, you may have running mates and can raise money as a ticket.* Some parties may finance your entire campaign; some may just give you a token amount and then you're on your own; and others, despite what they tell you, may be putting you up as a sure loser* and have already made a deal with the other side—so watch out!

Beware: Spending Your Money

Keep a close eye on how the party money is divvied up—you may end up on the short end of the stick.

Special Interests: There are numerous Political Action Committees (PACs),* organizations, clubs, and other groups that would help fund your race if you support their plank.* Some of the money the Clintons raise will go into special accounts associated with special interests. By doling out this money, they increase their power base and solidify their support. Wouldn't it be nice to receive a big check from the Clintons or one of the groups they funnel money to?

Real Life Scenario: The majority of people giving you money want something in return. Your neighbor wants a job for their kid. The contractor wants a contract. The special interests want you to be interested in them. And the party wants you to toe their line. A critical political skill is balancing all of these interests while still getting elected and maintaining your integrity. This is one of the more challenging parts of being an elected official.

Aside from vacuuming up every dollar you can, there are some other important considerations when it comes to campaign finance:

Follow the Rules: Since raising money is one of the most vital aspects of political life, you must play by the rules—and make sure you associate with people who know what the rules are. Your campaign account must be opened legally as per the laws pertaining to your particular office—your local board of elections can steer you in the right direction. You will also need checks printed with your campaign name and, hopefully, plenty of deposit slips.

You may be limited by law in how much money you can accept from individuals and corporations. Make sure you know what the limits are and stick to them. Don't get cute by having the developer of the mega mall max out on the corporate donation limit and then start funneling money to you through employees, etc. Or have the rich celebrity living next to the mall slip you a couple of grand in cash. This will get you in trouble and tank your campaign.

Keeping Track: As the money rolls in, you have to keep track of it and, in some cases, publically report it as per a fixed schedule. Don't screw this up because it can become a campaign issue. "How can we expect her to keep an eye on our tax dollars when she can't even keep her own books straight?" will be the first press release* put out by your opponent.

You will need people who you trust implicitly to handle your money. Appoint a Campaign Treasurer (preferably an accountant), perhaps a spouse or family member—someone you can count on outside of politics. Make sure they know what they're doing.

There is some strategy involved with reporting your finances. If you are raising a ton of money, make a big deal out of it to show the world you're serious. Don't blow all your money just before a reporting date so it looks like you're broke. Challenge your opponents to divulge their sources of income and make an issue out of what special interests are trying to buy them. Watch out: They will do the same to you.

> **Real Life Advice:** Your account name says a lot about you, so put some thought into it. "Friends of (Your Name)" implies you have a lot of friends giving you money. "The Committee to Stop the Mega Mall" gets right to the heart of the matter. Or you can get lofty with "Victory 2014" or "The So and So Campaign Team," etc. The last one is good if some of your running mates are proven money raisers and you link up with them.

If your funding is coming from your wealthy family, you can run free and clear of the special interests that have taken control of many elected bodies. If your opponent is using loads of family money, then he's a spoiled rich kid who's trying to buy the election. Either way, your ability to spin the issues will go a long way toward winning the war.

Budget: It's pretty despairing to chug along and then run out of money a few weeks before Election Day when it really counts. To prevent this calamity, create a budget. If your goal is to send a letter to every voter in your area, find out what it will cost for printing, letterhead, envelopes, and postage. If it costs $5,000 and you're on track to raise $4,000, you're in trouble. You can do the budget two ways: Estimate how much you can raise and then create a plan to spend it, or estimate what it will take to really make an impact and then go raise that amount. See the Appendix for a sample campaign budget.

Create a Backward Calendar: If you can only afford two letters, when will they hit the mail boxes? When should your radio spots air? Usually, the biggest impact will be closer to the election, so start from there and plan backwards. If your budget shows you can go into overdrive the week before Labor Day and your money will last until Election Day, you're probably in good shape. If you can only afford a single mailing the last week in October, then maybe it's time to hit the phones to scare up some additional funds.

Stay tuned for the next chapter to learn how you can raise money like the pros.

"There's just one more thing, honey," Mary said to her husband in her most agreeable tone.

"What's that?"

"I'd like to put up $1,000 of our money to get the campaign rolling. Would that be okay?"

"I guess that's alright. But where are you going to get the rest of it?"

"Rest assured. I have a plan."

Mary spent time at her desk laser-beam focused on the subject of raising money. She made a list of friends and family she could hit up, as well as business associates that would donate to the cause. There was an anti-tax group in town and the chamber of commerce chimes in from time to time when government spending issues come up.

She practiced on her neighbor, who was retired and pretty well to do.

"Hello Carol, it's Mary," she said cheerfully on the phone. "How's every going with you?"

Mary asked about her vacation and grandchildren, sewing circle and library project, and at the right moment, came out with her pitch:

"Carol, do you mind if I talk to you about something that's pretty important? You know how we're always complaining about high taxes and the town which never seems to do anything right? Well guess what? I'm going to run for the town council!"

"That's great. I've always wanted to live next to a big shot," Carol joked.

"Carol, can I ask you something, but if the answer is no that's okay, it's entirely up to you? Campaigns cost money and I'd like to ask you for a donation. Would that be okay?"

"Sure Mary. How much are we talking about?"

"Well, the individual limit for town campaigns is $6,500, but I'm not asking that much. Whatever you're comfortable with."

"How about $500?"

"That would be fantastic. Thank you very much. I really appreciate it. Carol, can I ask you one more favor? I know you know Bill across the street really well. Would it be asking too much if you could give him a call and let him know what we're up to, maybe see if he would like to donate too?"

"It would be my pleasure."

She hung up the phone thinking, *Carol would make a great Fundraising Coordinator.*

Mary got the donation because she made the call and asked. And she also asked if her neighbor could help her nail down even more donations. Because money is such a critical part of elections, Mary knows that she has to put time in her schedule to dial for dollars.* She has a plan to raise as much money as possible and wants to get a leg up on her opponents by concentrating on the almighty buck.

Mary gave Carol another piece of information that is also extremely important. She knew what the campaign limit was because she researched the election laws for her race. She opened a campaign account with her local bank (and hit up the bank president for a donation while she was at it) and filed the necessary paperwork with the board of elections under her new account, "Friends of Mary Morgan." She knows that nothing can sink a campaign faster than mishandling the money.

When she got home that night, Mary pulled out her calendar and started planning her campaign. She wanted to do at least one mailing per week in October and in the morning she was going to call her printer to find out how much they were going to cost, including postage. She was tired and wanted to go to bed, but spent a few extra minutes drafting her campaign plan so she could start on a budget. *If I have to raise money I should at least know how much,* she thought to herself. Before turning out the light she made a note to call her Uncle Saul, a CPA, to see if he would be her Campaign Treasurer.

CHAPTER FOUR

THE ART AND SCIENCE OF RAISING MONEY

4

The ability to raise campaign cash is priceless, so let's get right to it.

Contact Data Base: One of the Holy Grails of raising money is the Contact Data Base. Imagine if you had the names and numbers of 1,000 people who will each give you $100? You'd never lose.

If you are a staunch supporter of the Second Amendment (the right to bear arms), how'd you like the list of all the National Rifle Association members in your area? Or the Green Peace membership to air out your environmental plank? What about the people who signed the petition against the mega mall? We bet they'd kick in a few bucks if you were on their side.

Real Life Scenario: Right around the corner from Washington's hallowed halls of Congress are political offices with rows of cubicles and phones. These are not for lowly volunteers to dial for dollars, but the members of Congress themselves since the American taxpayers don't want them doing this from their government offices. Even the highest and mightiest must get on the phone and make The Ask—and do it often. No matter the office, the more you raise the better off you'll be, so don't be bashful about asking for the green.

This is what organized political machines work on every day. Donor lists have become highly specialized and are continually refined through computerized data bases. Don't be intimidated: your fundraising list can be a simple spreadsheet in your word processor. If you start lining up donors from day one and keep building your list, your data base will serve you well for the rest of your political life.

Real Life Scenario: We had the opportunity once to tour the warehouse where the Readers Digest contest entries are sent for recycling. You would be amazed at the huge mass of returned entries, floor to ceiling in a huge facility, all complete with the most vital information of the digest's trade: Valid names and addresses of future prospects well worth the millions of dollars they gave out to get them.

Programs such as Excel, Access, and Word—standard issue on most computers—can easily handle your data base. Essentials include name, mailing address, email, phone number, affiliation, man/woman, Republican/Democrat, etc. You can also note the campaign events they attended, how much they gave, check numbers, personal information for small talk, etc. The donation data will be in one convenient place if your race requires a financial report and the small talk notes will come in handy when you're dialing for dollars. The specific information will allow you to craft a special fundraising appeal just for them. The data base will also make it easy to send out thank yous.

Dialing for Dollars: With your list in hand, call people and ask them for money. Sounds simple, but it's hard to do unless you understand these basic principles, and then it's easy (and very lucrative).

A) Schedule time each week to dial for dollars and discipline yourself to stay on track.

B) Don't Go It Alone. Bring your campaign team in on the plan and have them make calls with you. Swear to each other that you will keep to the schedule. If they don't feel like doing it, make them, and vice versa.

C) Have Your Call Lists Ready To Go. The time you have scheduled to raise money is not to be used to look up phone numbers or talk about what you're going to say. If you have blocked out an hour to make calls, make calls—do not procrastinate.

D) Create a Script and Stick to It. Aside from small talk which will vary for each person you're calling, use the same language when you make your pitch. Once you've nailed down a script that works for you, burn it into your memory so you can deliver it naturally.

Seven Ingredients of an Effective Donation Pitch: Mary may not have realized it, but she used some very effective techniques when she asked her neighbor for money. If you make these Seven Ingredients part of your Donation Pitch, you should have no problem at all raising funds.

P.S. These ingredients work on the phone *and* face to face.

#1 Small Talk: Mary asked about the vacation, grand children, how the sewing circle was going, the library project, etc. and let Carol do most of the talking. It wasn't all about Mary.

#2 Get Serious: At the appropriate moment, Mary transitioned into the reason for the call and underscored its importance: "Carol, do you mind if I talk to you about something that's pretty important?"

#3 Get Permission: In the same sentence, Mary also asked for Carol's permission to continue. Of course she said "yes" and this set up Mary to get another "yes" later on when she asked the big question. Asking smaller questions leading up to the big one is an effective strategy, don't you think?

#4 Set It Up: "You know how we're always complaining about high taxes and the town which never seems to do anything right?" Mary asked, causing Carol to ruminate on some of the things that bother her about local government.

On cue, Mary went to her next point: "Well guess what? I'm going to run for the town council!" This was the **#5 Attention-Getting Announcement** that got Carol caught up in the moment.

#6 The Ask: The techniques Mary used leading up to this critical moment made it easy: "Carol, can I ask you something, but if the answer is no that's okay, it's entirely up to you? Campaigns cost money and I'd like to ask you for a donation. Would that be okay?"

"How about $500?" Carol replied. Bingo!

#7 Branches: Mary knows that people who give to a cause are "buying in" and would approach people they know to donate as well—if only you ask them.

"Carol, can I ask you one more favor? I know you know Bill across the street really well. Would it be asking too much if you could give him a call and let him know what we're up to, maybe see if he would like to donate too?"

Making a "warm call" where you already have a connection is much more effective than a "cold call." So if Carol called Bill first and Mary followed up with him, she would have a much better chance of getting a donation than if she called Bill out of the blue.

The Mail Merge:* If you received a personally addressed letter on an issue that concerns you, would you be inclined to send a check? What if the letter came from someone you know or a big-name celebrity or local personality and it appealed directly to you?

A mail merge program takes lists of personal data and merges it into letters that seem like they were written exclusively for the recipient. You can also print envelopes, mailing labels, call lists, thank yous—anything requiring a personal touch—using the mail merge as well.

Direct Mail Pitch: Your data base will enable you to distribute one of the more powerful money-raising tools, the Direct Mail Pitch. In your most impassioned, personal, and direct prose, draft a letter about you, your campaign, and why people should care. Tell them what you're going to do for them. At the end, ask for money, and don't forget a P.S. reiterating your main points

Real Life Scenario: When he first ran for the U.S. Senate, Al D'Amato's secret weapon was his elderly mom whose homespun letters to senior citizens meant the difference in the race. In fact, she became a celebrity on the campaign trail talking about recipes, senior issues, and most importantly, her son.

and how important their donation will be to advance these concerns. If the letter is going to the family, friends, and neighbors listed in your data base, write like you are talking directly to them. If you're writing to the opponents of the mega mall, tell them how you will stop it if elected. Tell the NRA crowd how you loved hunting as a youth and why you'll never let them mess with your right to bear arms. The more focused your mailings are to the groups receiving them, the more successful you will be.

The fundraising letter doesn't have to be from you. The president of the Citizens Against the Mega Mall can send out a letter on your behalf or your mom, the mayor, Arnold Schwarzenegger, or whoever you can get who has standing with the group you are writing to. Candidates use direct appeals from former senators, celebrities, and public figures all the time. Why not put them to work for you?

Real Life Scenario: Some campaigns use the actions of their opponents as money making tools. In the lead up to the 2008 presidential primary, Hillary Clinton's campaign sent out a fund-raising appeal to make money off heated exchanges between Clinton and Barack Obama. The message was basically: "Now that I'm being attacked by my opponent on such and such issue, please send me money to continue fighting the good fight."

Your direct mail letter should look like this:

Mary Morgan
77 Main Street
Centerville, Ohio, 45458

June 16, 2014

Mr. Walter P. Johnson
12 Oak Avenue
Centerville, Ohio 45458

Dear Mr. Johnson:

Why does the town keep raising taxes while we get <u>fewer services?</u>

And why did they approve a huge condo development along the river that will put more and more kids in the school district to <u>drive up taxes even further?</u>

It should come as no surprise that people are upset when:

- **We are forced to pay some of the highest taxes in the nation.**
- **Senior citizens can't afford to live here anymore.**
- **Once we pay dearly to educate our children, they leave Centerville because there are no jobs here.**
- **The town council gave themselves another raise and put five more patronage employees on the payroll.**

Mr. Johnson, we need new leadership at town hall and I'm writing to let you know that after considering the matter very seriously—and coming to the conclusion I can do a better job for the taxpayers—I am running for the town council.

continued

Here's my promise to you:

- **I will make sure every public dollar is accounted for and will not raise taxes.**
- **I will create a business-friendly atmosphere to attract new companies to Centerville and create jobs.**
- **I will make sure we get all of the government services we pay for.**
- **I will subject all housing development plans to environmental *and* economic review to make sure they don't overtax our resources.**
- **I will not create any new political positions at town hall and will freeze the salaries of all political appointees.**

Our municipal workers do a good job…

…but they are hampered by poor budgeting, misspent resources, and a lack of leadership from our elected officials.

Dr. Morton Blackstein, economics professor at Centerville College, said it best:

"Centerville can see better days if we put our high tax and political problems behind us. If there ever was a need for new leadership at town hall, it is now."

What does this mean for you? Less government spending and lower taxes will help pull our town out of its economic slump and make living here more affordable. Our seniors will be more comfortable and there will be more good-paying jobs for our youth and middle class. We will get the services we deserve allowing Centerville to rebound and once again be a place we can be proud

continued

to call home.

Mr. Johnson, will you help me break the cycle of bad politics at town hall and get our economy back on track? Your generous donation of $10, $25, $100, $1,000 or more would be an enormous help in making a change for the better.

Together, I'm confident we can make Centerville a more vibrant and affordable place to live. Whatever donation you can afford will go a long way toward starting the turnaround so many of us have been clamoring for. Thank you.

Sincerely,

Mary Morgan

Candidate, Centerville Town Council

P.S. The town council proposed a budget with **another 4% tax increase.** Aren't we already taxed to death? Say no to high taxes. Fill out the donor card and return it in the enclosed envelope today. Thank you.

There are a few important points to note about Mary's letter:

- It's on the candidate's letterhead and comes in a matching envelope with Mary's name and return address in Centerville.
- It's addressed specifically to the recipient and uses his name throughout the text.
- It starts with an attention-getting question (and follows up with one as well).
- It also poses questions throughout.
- It sums up the problems and offers the candidate's promises as solutions.
- It spells out "What does this mean for you?"
- It covers numerous "hot button" issues.
- It quotes a trusted source.
- It asks for a donation and suggests amounts from $10 to $1,000 or more.
- It thanks the potential donor.
- It uses a P.S. to make another point and ask again for a donation.
- It includes a donation card stating clearly who to make the checks out to, as well as a pre-addressed return envelope.
- It underlines and bolds key phrases and uses lines separated by... for emphasis.

While the letter takes the current administration to task, it praises the town workers since there's no sense picking a fight with them. Plus, the candidate will have to work with these employees upon getting elected.

Mary's platform in taking on the town council is evident throughout the letter. Whatever your issues are, make a compelling case using the techniques outlined above.

One final thought: Make a budget decision on whether or not to put postage on the return envelopes based on the size of the mailing and how likely the recipients will be to respond.

The Fundraising Event: People want to press the flesh with candidates they perceive as winners and will pay good money to do so. A fundraising event is where you will interact with your stakeholders and hear what issues are important to them. They are paying to see you, so spend some quality time with them. It also gives you a friendly environment to air out your stump speech.

Staging a successful event is a team effort, so don't go it alone. Discuss the details with your staff and keep checklists so nothing falls through the cracks. Like any important endeavor, you'll need people who can follow through and you must supervise them to make sure they stay on track.

Let's jump right into it:

Set the Location, Time and Date: Avoid holidays and check around first for conflicting events. Weekdays from 6 p.m. to 8 p.m. work well because they give people getting off work time to get there and you won't be infringing on their weekends. If it's an anti-mega mall rally/fundraiser, a Saturday morning would be okay.

Decide if you are serving **food**—buffet, hors d'oeuvres, beverages, etc. Put some thought into whether or not you want to serve alcohol.

Print tickets, mailing envelopes, return envelopes, and RSVP response cards. Include a solicitation letter which can be from you or someone making an appeal on your behalf such as your Fundraising Coordinator, running mate or someone associated with one of you causes such as the president of the Committee to Stop the Mega Mall. A celebrity or well-known personality would also get people's attention, as would a popular elected official.

> **Bonus:** Have your solicitation letter come from a committee and list all the members down the side to show you have some oomph. List them down the other side as well if you have that many.

Who to Invite? Start with your database and make it a point to keep expanding it. Call your friends and supporters and ask them for names and addresses of potential donors. Go over your platform and contact groups that share your views. If you are running with the support of an organization, see if you can get their list or a set of mailing labels. If they say they will send something out for you, stay on them to make sure they do.

Promo: Post the event on your website and Social Media such as your Facebook page. Tweet it. Set it up so people can buy tickets online through a service such as Eventbrite.com or ThrdPlace.com. Send out at least three emails: One announcing the event, a reminder (or two) and another announcing something special like a celebrity showing up or a high office holder. Make sure your email features some nice graphics, the event ticket perhaps, and not just verbiage like you'd see in a regular message. Email services such as Constant Contact, Mail Chimp, Campaigner, and Elite Mail have some nice templates you can use. There's more on Social Media and effective emailing later in this guide.

You can run an ad in the local papers or even send a press release or letter to the editor announcing the fundraiser with a little verbiage on why you're running and what your race is about.

Theme: Consider a theme such as a campaign kickoff, Fourth of July bonanza, end of summer gala, clam bake, birthday celebration, block party, etc. Have some fun with it.

Remind and Hound: After your mailing goes out, schedule your staff to follow up by telephone. Provide them with a script on exactly what you want them to say. Your potential donors will be turned off if they're approached by someone with poor phone skills. Go with something like this:

Hello Mr. Smith. This is Jane Murray calling for Mary Morgan. How are you today?

The reason for my call is I'm following up on Mary's invitation to her fundraiser on May 16. Did you receive it? (If no, offer to send them another and then tell them what it's about).

There are a lot of us working pretty hard for Mary because we're confident she will make the changes we need at town hall. Mr. Smith, can we count on your support as well? Great. That's wonderful. Thank you very much. I know Mary will be happy to see you. Will you be bringing a guest on the 16th or will it just be you? Thank you. We'll make sure there's room for you.

As the candidate, don't be afraid to get your hands dirty and make some calls, especially to the big bucks donors who will buy a table of 10. Send out some personal emails.

Have your team keep a running estimate of RSVP's to provide to the caterer. An accurate head count will help you save money on food.

VIP's–Make sure you invite your running mates, officials from the organizations backing you, and other VIP's. Write "Complimentary" on their tickets since the more bigwigs you have the more successful you will appear. At the event, make sure a staffer makes a list of the VIP's as they come in so you don't forget anyone when you make your speech.

The Setting: If you are only expecting 100 people, don't book a room that holds 500 or your event will look like a failure. Put up appropriate decorations such as balloons, bunting, posters, etc. Put out stacks of your brochures and campaign handouts such as pens, pads, etc. Circulate a sign-up sheet to get people's contact information for your database. Better yet, give away a prize like a new TV where people have to fill out a ticket to win.

> **Real Life Scenario:** When President Bush gave his "Mission Accomplished" speech on the aircraft carrier Abraham Lincoln his advance people made sure there was a stunning backdrop of military personnel and weaponry behind him. Remember, it's not just your talking head in the picture that counts, but what's around you, so make your surroundings as impressive as possible.

You will need a podium and a nice backdrop for your speech. Expect to be photographed and videoed, so make sure the podium has a sign on it with your name and campaign slogan. Are you having a DJ?

Logistics: Give the event a once-through with your staff and try to think of everything that could go wrong. What time is the caterer showing up? Will there be enough parking? Do the bathrooms have toilet paper? Little things can make you look bad and create a negative impression of your management skills.

Work the Room: Get there early and greet your guests as they come in. Shake hands and personally thank them for coming. Make sure the line doesn't back up. When everybody's in, circulate around the room; visit each table. Ask how people are, their families;

Real Life Scenario: How many times have you been to an event and the microphone squeals or the people in the back can't hear? This is embarrassing and will reflect badly on you. So make sure the sound system is working in advance. "Sound check, 1-2-3!"

show interest. Smile a lot. Laugh. Glad hand.* Slap backs. Have a photographer take grin and grab photos of you and your guests. Also take some candid shots of you engrossed in conversation which you can use for your campaign literature.

Keep in mind that some of your guests will be **working you.** Donors will be looking for something in return, so be prepared to absorb what they are saying and keep track of it. Scribble on one of your pads (with a nice pen). This is one of the most basic tenets of the political process, so learn how to deal with it. Some will want a separate meeting and if they're a big donor or represent a major issue, set it up on the spot. Many will offer advice and give you words of wisdom on campaign strategy and the pressing issues of the day. Be a good listener—after all, they paid to communicate with you. Have your wing man move you along if someone gets too long winded.

Program: About half way through, have an emcee get everyone's attention and start the program. The emcee should be one of the biggest cheeses in the room, a local celebrity or maybe the chairman of the committee to stop the mega mall.

If there are other VIP's who want to talk, have the emcee call them up. The emcee should say a few brief words about how great the campaign is going and how important it is to get you elected. Give them a brief preamble they can use to introduce you.

Your Speech: Prepare and practice what you're going to say ahead of time and try not to read from a piece of paper. This is a good time for you to polish your oratory skills with a friendly crowd. If you're nervous, picture them in their underwear.

Thank everyone who helped organize the event—volunteers, ticket sellers, the caterer. Recognize your family, the kids, and make sure you say a "Honey-I-couldn't-do-this-without-you" for the significant other. Be sincere and heartfelt. Go to your VIP list and acknowledge them.

Mention that there are so many important people in attendance that you may have forgotten a few, so apologize to them in advance so they don't feel slighted.

Be brief on the issues and close with how important everyone's support will be on Election Day. For dramatic effect, call your family and staff up on the stage. Wave while the confetti drops. This, too, will make a great campaign photo.

At the end, stand by the door and thank everyone on their way out. Again, make sure the line doesn't back up—people want to go home!

After the event, update your data base and send all contributors and attendees a thank you note signed by you personally. If there are too many to sign, consider yourself lucky and start signing. For those who gave a lot, write a brief note on how much they mean to you. Also, don't forget follow up appointments with those who asked to see you (and don't be bashful in asking for even more money).

Finally, make sure your Treasurer keeps track of who gave what for the purposes of making necessary reports. It goes without saying, but make sure they get the money in the bank.

Email Campaigning: Online marketing revolves around one thing: Getting people's email address so you can pitch them. These techniques work extremely well for campaign fundraising and email has become a vital money tool. Don't believe us? Go to the website of your favorite party and sign up. Almost immediately you will receive a never-ending barrage of clever email pitches. These will be very educational for you since they raise tons of money and you can see how the experts do it.

The successful email campaign starts with a robust list. Build yours from the ground up adding friends and supporters and everyone you meet. Make it a point to collect email addresses in whatever you do.

Real Life Scenario: When the president was pitching the benefits of Obamacare during his State of the Union Address, Congressman Joe Wilson of South Carolina shouted, "You lie." The incident gained national attention and was quickly made part of email pitches by the Republicans. They raised millions with it.

Use an email hosting service instead of your free Yahoo or Google mail. They have nice-looking templates you can use for exactly this purpose and have help centers that will walk you through step by step. The emails should have icons linking to your website, Social Media, and a place where people can safely donate using their credit card. You can import email addresses right from your donor database and the hosting system will manage them by eliminating duplicates and weeding out bad ones. The system will also provide statistics on rejects, opens and clicks to places such as your website and fundraiser. Email is required to have an opt-out button and the service will automatically remove people who choose not to hear from you.

> **Bonus:** Setting a fundraising goal and using it to spur your contributors creates excitement, especially if the goal is something they can relate to: "We need to raise only $1,500 more to print 5,000 anti-mega mall flyers. Won't you help spread our message that this monstrosity is just too big for our area?" Call it a "Money Bomb" fundraiser and set a deadline to print the flyers. Check out **www.WinAnElection.org** for all kinds of examples.

Plan a series of emails and don't hit people up for money at first. Instead, offer them something of interest like a rundown of the issues, town hall update or an article about the race. This is where your creativity will shine and put you on par with the Internet pros who devote huge brainpower toward keeping their messages relevant and thought provoking. For your donation emails, include a box where people can click to send money. Again, Constant Contact and the other services provide the mechanisms including an automated thank you note. To see how it's done, go online and pony up a few bucks to a major cause.

You can also take a page out of Congressman Wilson's book. While you don't have to call the president a liar, you can generate a hot topic of your own and send out a solicitation based around it. Another idea is to set a goal and keep sending out updates and appeals until it's reached. Take another look at the direct mail letter earlier in this chapter. You can use the same verbiage and techniques for your email appeal.

Special Interests: Government is overrun by special interests, or so the criticism goes, and there's a reason why people think that way. Money talks and B.S. walks and there are any number of businesses, groups, and organizations that will help fund your race if you come down on their side. PACs are set up specifically for this purpose and lobbyists and insiders make fortunes by facilitating the flow of money to the people in power. Why not let it be you?

Real Life Scenario: The Democratic National Committee won't let you into their website unless you type in your email address and once you do, the next screen that pops up says this:

Thanks for adding your name. President Obama called on all of us to make 2014 a year of action, but it's up to Democrats to get the job done.

We're going to be fighting to support the President's agenda and stop Republican obstructionism.

But we can't do it without you. Chip in to support Democrats today.

Beware: There's a word for unwanted email solicitations—Spam

Sending messages to people you don't know or who didn't sign up to receive them will get you kicked off the Internet. That's why most websites have email capture systems and pop ups that ask you to Join the Team, Are You In?, Send Me More, etc. Email services will keep track of spam reports and will notify you if there are too many.

CAMPAIGN UPDATE

Mary was ecstatic. Her neighbor, Carol, agreed to be her Fundraising Coordinator and they got together the next morning to plan. The first order of business was a fundraising event and it was obvious that Carol was in her element.

"We'll hold it at Umberto's on Main Street from six to eight," Carol announced. "I checked around and it looks like nothing's happening on May 16, so we'll go with that date. Mary, how's that print shop you used for your business cards?"

"Great. I'll go see them later to get the tickets started."

"No, you have too much to do. Let me handle that," Carol said, confirming in Mary's mind that she made an excellent choice in bringing her aboard. "I know the manager over at Umberto's pretty well and we'll put together a checklist of everything we need to do."

It turns out, Carol's nephew, Bernard, was into online marketing and he showed up at the meeting.

"Do you have a website set up yet?" Bernard asked.

"No."

"Facebook page?"

"No."

"Blog? Email service? Twitter account? Online event ticketing?"

"No and nope."

"No problem. I can do it all." He looked at Carol.

"Bernard's a pro, so he needs to get paid," Carol told the candidate. "But don't worry, I'll make sure we have enough money in the budget for him and the Campaign Manager."

"Fine with me. Great to have you aboard," Mary said, shaking Bernard's hand.

In a few days, Bernard set up a website with some nice graphics, flattering head shot of Mary and pictures of her talking to some seniors and local businessmen. Bernard created a logo with an American flag and incorporated a red, white and blue theme throughout. The site featured her bio and bullet points from her platform. It had a big box linking to the fundraiser and was set up so you could buy tickets online. There was a "Join Mary" email signup section and a row of icons for Facebook, LinkedIn, Blog, and Twitter. There was also a tab for Latest News, Join the Team where people could sign up to volunteer, and information about the town.

Mary clicked one of the icons and was transported to her Facebook page. Bernard had set up an "event" for the fundraiser which included a link to the page where people could buy tickets.

She already had 100 likes on Facebook.

Bernard had showed her how to make a post.

"I'm heading to the town council meeting tonight to speak out on the tax hike," Mary wrote. "Won't you join me at 7 p.m.?"

She was afraid to push the button to post it and called Carol.

"I'm so nervous she told her. This is my first post."

"Go ahead. People want to know what's going on."

Mary hit the button.

"I did it!"

"Good going."

"Wow! What's this?" Mary's post already had a like— one of their neighbors.

"Joan's onboard!"

CHAPTER FIVE
TAKING THE PULSE OF THE VOTERS

5

Knowing what people are thinking is critical Intel for an election campaign. While it's hard to draw a conclusion from the opinion of just a few, an accurate picture can be drawn from sampling a large group (plus or minus a few percentage points, as the pollsters say). Depending on how they are handled, polls can be valuable or downright confusing. For a race large enough to afford it, a good professional pollster can produce information you can use to fine-tune your message and your strategy. In a smaller race, your own research—talking to voters, volunteers, civics, supporters—will give you a good idea of the issues that will drive the election. You can tap your team or a think tank to ferret out the hot topics and also use an online service such as Survey Monkey to tap into the minds of the electorate.

Real Life Advice: A knowledgeable candidate is the best candidate. Your grasp on the issues by reading the newspapers, attending meetings, research, polling, talking to people, etc. will make you well armed in the battle for your seat.

Let's start with the types of polls and how you can use the results to win.

Issues Research or Benchmark polls seek to find out what major issues are driving the voters and how you rate with them. You may think the majority is concerned about the mega mall, but maybe not. Maybe they're more worried about economic development and finding work. For example, a poll of 500 likely voters determined the top issues as follows:

- 35% Economic development
- 25% Job creation
- 20% Reduce taxes
- 10% Environmental protection
- 10% Other

Another question revealed:

- 77% favor the Mega mall
- 23% oppose the Mega mall

So if the majority of the sampled voters are in favor of the mega mall and if you are running as a mall opponent, you're in trouble. Because the poll shows that people are worried about their financial well-being, it would be wise to have a strong economic plank.

You might ask where the pollster focused the survey: People living near the mall or in different parts of the town? Did they question more men than women? Retirees or workers? The bottom line is that a professional pollster can fine tune results as precisely as your budget will allow. On top of that, they should be able to advise you on how your campaign should take best advantage of the data.

Real Life Advice: Polls can be written to conclude pretty much anything you want. If you want to show that your opponent is weak on the issues and the voters don't trust him, a "poll" can be written to accommodate those sentiments.

Your polls will involve two types of data: The basic results and the cross tabs, which is a demographic analysis of the people being polled and what they're thinking. For example, you may have a better favorable rating than your opponent, but among whom? Women may go for you at a higher percentage than men, but with senior women, you're not so good. Or you're up with young people, but not those who consider themselves as conservative. The same with issues: men may be more concerned with jobs vs. environmental matters than women. Make sure your pollster knows how to break it all down and then provide guidance on how your campaign should approach these voting groups.

A key part of your poll should be questions about you and your opponent. How would you like to find that out of 500 voters surveyed, 42% have a favorable opinion of you, 38% side with your opponent and 20% haven't made up their minds yet? Of the people who like you, a majority are women while men are leaning toward your opponent. Senior citizens make up the bulk of the undecided. With this intelligence, you can form a road map for your campaign—for example, communicate heavily with the women to make sure they stay with you and hone in on the undecided seniors. As for the men who back your opponent, break it down even further: Only the men who consider themselves conservatives support your opponent while liberals are undecided.

What if 65% of people under age 40 say they never heard of you? With younger generations getting most of their information online these days, this tells you to ramp up your Internet-related activities such as Social Media and online advertising.

After a month or so on the campaign trail following your first poll, you will want to do a...

Tracking Poll: This should tell you if your efforts to shore up your base* are working and if you're getting traction with the undecideds and younger voters. The tracking polls let you know what's working and what's not and where you have to double down or just give up on certain voter groups entirely so as not to waste your resources.

For the tracking, let's say you campaigned hard against the mega mall for a solid month. Your bench mark poll had your approval rating on the issue at 60% percent and now your tracking poll shows it at 70%. Now you know you're getting somewhere!

Polls as a Campaign Weapon: Let's say a poll shows your opponent getting creamed by the women's vote. Send out a press release and let the world know (but be prepared to show your poll results in case your opponent challenges your findings). Or what if your favorables* jumped a few points between tracking polls. Let your donors know how well you're doing and ask them for more money. You could also do a **Push Poll,** phone calls that masquerade as a survey, but use questions designed to cast your opponent in a bad light.

Real Life Advice: Some polling firms do the bulk of their business in the even numbered years when state and federal candidates run. In the off years,* they will be inclined to charge less for their services to keep business up.

Bonus: Some tips on negotiating price with a pollster:

- The cost of making phone calls is relatively fixed and the business comes with a high mark up, so if the price seems high, it's probably because your pollster's trying to make a killing. Contact different firms, check their credentials, and negotiate downward.

- Your initial meeting with a pollster will be a sales pitch, so try to focus the conversation on what exactly the pollster will do for you and for how much. Be aware that for every question you want to add to the poll, the pollster will want to increase the price.

- Find out what kind of consultation you will receive from the actual poll results. As part of their fee, the pollster should be at your side in making decisions about strategy, message, mailing, advertising, etc. In fact, many like to do package deals where they also handle your outreach, so make sure you get specific about available services and costs.

CAMPAIGN UPDATE

Mary's fundraising was going well and her Campaign Manager, Rob (we'll formally introduce him a little later), convinced her to do some polling. After interviewing several firms, including one Rob worked with previously, they decided to go with the company he was familiar with.

It was an off year—there were few state or congressional races—so the vice president of the company agreed to do a baseline poll and three tracking polls at a reduced rate. For each, they were going to survey 250 people and ask 10 questions, in addition to the demographic data—male/female, age, etc. Rob went over the details to make sure the results and cross tabs would give them viable information they could use to fine-tune Mary's position on the issues and her mailing campaign.

Rob knew that so early in the race, voters had little to go on and the poll results would probably show Mary as pretty much an unknown. But he had an ulterior motive: He wanted to arm Mary with some favorable stats to show potential supporters. Mary was a Democrat and they had heard two other names for the Democratic nomination: Donald Fink, a political appointee on the Centerville Industrial Development Agency, and Madeline Shott, a perennial candidate* who's never actually won anything.

The pollster went to work and was very selective about who was surveyed. They focused the bulk of the calls in Mary's part of town and called more women than men. The strategy did the trick and Mary's poll showed her with a slight edge over Fink and Shott. The survey also gave them valuable data on what people think about town hall and the issues, especially their dim view on government spending and taxes. They found out the citizenry is pretty much split over the mega mall with people living closer to it much more opposed than those in other parts of the district. It showed the incumbent, Republican Frank Amato, had better name recognition*—they already knew that—but also had a high unfavorable rating among certain groups. He could be beat.

CHAPTER SIX
GETTING THE NOD

6

There's no question that established political parties and special interest groups get their candidates elected time after time. The question is: How do you get them to endorse you?

The Silver Spoon Method: Similar to inheriting "Old Money," you can find yourself born into a political dynasty and capitalize handsomely on your family connections.

People love to back a sure thing and will go for a familiar name. A son, daughter or wife can easily take over for a successful politician. This instant name recognition, as well as built-in party support, fundraising, and access to a network years in the making, can give you a huge leg up. So, if you're the offspring of a local power broker or the scion of a family such as the Bushes or Kennedys, you're already surrounded by people who can make things happen for you. For the rest of us, we'll have to go out and earn it.

Real Life Scenario: Former President George W. Bush and his brother, Jeb Bush, past governor of Florida, are perfect examples of inheriting power. Their father, President George H.W. Bush, had the connections, experience, fame, and know how—not to mention the name recognition and money sources—to help them scale the heights of government. Even a grandson, George P. Bush, is in politics running for Texas Land Commissioner.

The Parties Go On: Quite often, candidates are groomed as part of a farm team by party bosses. They keep their political machines running by putting the party faithful* in office and may look to you as another cog in their wheel. This is not necessarily a bad thing since their support could land you in an enterprise that controls millions, if not billions, of taxpayer dollars.

Beware: Nepotism*

An opponent may stoke public resentment over family members promoting each other and look to put an end to your dynasty (or you can put an end to theirs).

Joining a party and working your way up through the ranks is a time-tested way of making it to the top. The powers that be may start you off by getting you appointed to an open seat. Many times, these positions are vacated by persons who are "promoted" to run for a higher office, a great way to climb the political ladder. Running as an incumbent with experience on the job, albeit as an appointee, gives you a nice head start when it's time to face the voters.

Real Life Scenario: The Democrat machine in Chicago is a classic example of a political organization controlling government in order to perpetuate itself. Richard J. Daley served as mayor for 21 years and his son, Richard M. served decades more—a multi-generational dynasty built by controlling the public purse.

A Quick Note on Appointments: After you're seated, you may be required to run during the next scheduled election or in a special election* called specifically for your position. This means you'll have an election breathing down your neck as soon as you take office. A way to avoid this is to be appointed to fill an unexpired term. If the previous office holder won a four-year seat and left after only a year, you could get to serve the remaining three years before having to run. In politics, these considerations come into play a great deal when deciding how and when party members are promoted and their open seats filled.

Start Small: A great way to break into politics is getting yourself appointed to a non-elected position such as a deputy or assistant and, after a few years of dedicated service, go after your party's nod for an elected seat. Depending on how you play the game, you could move rapidly up the food chain and one day find yourself in Congress, as many have done. Grooming party standard bearers* this way is a tried and true method of perpetuating the machine.

Real Life Scenario: The first woman elected to the U.S. Senate was Hattie Wyatt Caraway of Arkansas. She was appointed in 1931 to fill the vacancy caused by the death of her husband, Senator Thaddeus Caraway, and then won an election for the seat.

The established political parties stay in power by cultivating voting blocs,* amassing campaign workers, mastering election law and, most importantly, raising money to carry the day for their candidates. These factors can be so powerful it's been joked quite seriously that some candidates would be better off going on vacation for the duration of the campaign and not risk doing something stupid that could cost them the race.

History of the Office: It pays to know something about the office you seek and the politics surrounding it. Has it always been controlled by a particular party? Are you a round Republican trying to fit into a square Democratic hole? A historical perspective will enable you to better assess your chances and tailor your approach to fit the circumstances. A little research just may give you an edge when you seek the support of the powers that be or wage a war against them.

Other Races: Perhaps the seat you covet is not a typical government position. You could be vying for a spot on the school board, your union, or the water district where there is no Republican vs. Democrat. The tactics and strategies are pretty much the same. You'll have to know the particulars of the election and who you'll need to connect with to build your base.*

If you want to knock off your union president, find out what's bugging the workers and who's leading the malcontents. If school taxes keep going up, make yourself an expert on the budget and take a shot at the board of ed. And if your sights are set on a panel that does business behind closed doors, or-ganize the aggrieved and run on an Open Government ticket.

For every office, there's a power base working to maintain the status quo. And for every status quo, there's a group bucking for change. If you're serious about running for something, you should get to know who's who.

For example, the Teacher's Union has a lot riding on the school board race; so does the Superintendent's Association. There's also the Senior Citizens Against Taxes and the newly-formed Students for Better Education which is against cuts to after-school programs and sports. And then there's the PTA which naturally gravitates toward the teachers since parents want what's best for their kids. Maybe this time it's different. A sleeping giant has been awakened. The 63 percent of the people who didn't bother to vote the last time are stirring. Some want new blood, some want the status quo, some want more spending, some want less. Why should they vote for you?

A Friend Indeed: Often, it's not what you know, it's who you know. Perhaps you have a close friend or neighbor who's risen through the political ranks and has a seat at the table. Maybe they would help promote you up the political ladder. Many an elected official has been taken under a wing and flown up through the ranks by a power broker friend. Keep in mind, however, for every benevolent soul that would help you, there are 10 more that see you as a threat to their favorite son and will try to shoot you down. Your friend's enemies will be your enemies.

Who's Got the Power? It pays to know how organizations are structured and who's got the power to make or break you. The most basic political official in some states is the party committee member or delegate. Research the local political system to see how it's done in your area and how much these people are actually involved in deciding who their group supports.

Theoretically, delegates select candidates during conventions. We say theoretically, because the rank and file rarely gets to make the final decision. Party bosses or a small inner circle usually controls the process and the conventions are a mere formality.

Sometimes, the decision will go to the "floor" making for an interesting political display as the candidates vie in an open forum. Some areas do it through straw polls and other mechanisms, so find out how it's done for your seat.

Real Life Scenario: "Don't worry kid, we're behind you a 100 percent," the big shot power broker says to you a few minutes after he just told your opponent the same thing. It's the oldest trick in the book: Why risk supporting the loser when you can promise them both?

If anointing candidates was really a fair and open process, it would work something like this: The powers that be would invite all interested candidates to submit their resumes and appear before a screening committee. The committee would select their favorites and make recommendations. A general meeting would be held and the members of the organization would get to vote on the recommended candidates. If you didn't make it past the screening committee, you could take your case to the convention floor and appeal directly to the membership to win your party's nomination.

To get the process going, let the organization's leadership know you would like their support. Call or write them a letter or both. Try to get an introduction from someone who's connected. Get a meeting.

The group leader may not be the only person in the room, so reach out to the executive committee, directors, vice chairs, zone leaders, committee members, etc. If they're willing to support you, ask if they will contact other decision makers on your behalf. The goal is to wrap up the process in your favor before the party even begins the screening process.

Money Talks: A big ace up your sleeve can be a major financial supporter. If Mr. Money Bags calls the chairman on your behalf and pledges a hefty dose of the magic word, your candidacy could take off faster than you can say "inside track."

The next important group to consider is your potential **running mates**. Start with the incumbents. Let them know what you bring to the table and make sure your platform jibes with theirs. Get a commitment if you can and let the world know. Nothing is more impressive at a screening committee meeting than walking in as the favorite of the home team.

If you are not the favorite son or daughter, you'll find out soon enough. If you've made a good impression, but are not chosen, negotiate for a different seat or position, maybe an appointed job or even a raise or promotion if you're already in the system. Rather than have a fight on their hands, the leadership may very well toss you a bone to keep you from causing them extra work.

Primary Elections: There is still hope for your candidacy if the party bosses don't see things your way–the primary election.* Simply put: you are now taking your case directly to the enrolled voters of your party. Depending on the rules in your area, you will have to qualify to get on the primary ballot and will run in an election against the candidate(s) chosen by the party. These are some of the more divisive elections in the political process because they pit party members vs. party members. See Chapter Ten for more on primary elections.

Most times, you face an uphill battle in a primary because you are bucking the professional politicians and their minions who have the resources, money, and skill to defeat you. But every once in a while, a heavy hand by the bosses can work in your favor if the rank and file is tired of having candidates selected for them. The party committee members or delegates may not rock the boat during the selection process for fear of repercussions from the leadership, but when it comes time to deliver the vote, you may have a nice surprise in store and find yourself on the winning side of an internal conflict.

> **Real Life Scenario:** Governor Mitt Romney learned a valuable lesson in the Republican primary election in his bid to unseat President Barak Obama. To woo conservative voters, he had to lean to the right. He then had to track back to the middle to attract general election votes. His readjusting on issues became an albatross around his neck, a fact Obama trumpeted frequently in defeating him.

Defeating the party candidate in a primary can be a mixed blessing. The leadership could be so angered they make a deal with the other side in the general election* and your goose is cooked.

Steal Their Thunder: Another strategy is going after endorsements your opponent has taken for granted. Maybe a group is open to a new face and since your opponent hasn't kissed their ring lately, you could pick up their support. Or, maybe you're already a member of an organization and you convince them to nominate one of their own instead. Couple this support with a few other groups and you just may emerge as the frontrunner. Many an incumbent has gone down in flames because they didn't cater to their supporters and got outfoxed.

A New Party: As a staunch opponent of the mega mall, you could create a new party line, Citizens Against the Mega Mall, for example, and make your own endorsement. If hundreds of voters have risen up against the mall, they may vote for you even if you're a Democrat and they're a Republican. These extra supporters could very well provide your margin of victory. Other groups could be Citizens for Lower Taxes, if taxes are a big issue in your area, or the Senior Rights Party, if you are pursuing an older voting bloc.

Split the Vote: You could also encourage another candidate to run with views similar to your opponent and split the vote. The third choice, or spoiler,* would dilute your opponent's base and give you the advantage.

Real Life Scenario: U.S. Senator Joe Lieberman of Connecticut, former vice presidential candidate on the Al Gore ticket, former congressman, former state attorney general, and holder of his vaunted senate seat for more years than you can count got knocked off in a Democratic primary election by a political unknown grousing about the senator's support of the Iraq war. Incredibly, Lieberman ran in the general election as an independent and, with plenty of the great equalizer, money, won reelection.

Real Life Scenario: Democrats in the Texas State House cried foul over the 2000 census and the way it was used to realign election districts. With the stroke of a pen, the party in power, which happened to be the GOP, eliminated state legislature seats that were held by Democrats. How's that for consolidating power? Just get rid of your opponents' seats. In order to pass the new Gerrymandered* districts into law, the legislature needed a quorum which the Republicans could not obtain unless a certain amount of Democrats were present. So the Donkeys did what any hard-ball politicians would do: they left town. And the Elephants chased them. It went as far as arrest warrants being issued for Democrats who actually left the country by slipping over the border to Mexico. What a mess! But a sterling example of just how far the existing power structures will go to hold on to their juice.

Three Strikes and You're Not Out: Losing an election is not necessarily a bad thing, particularly if you're new at it. While you may not pick up enough votes to win, your effort will give you experience, name recognition, and a better chance next time. And who's to say the person who beat you is any better? If the bum screws up (or is mired in scandal or dies or who knows what), you will be the frontrunner based simply on the fact that you ran for the seat before. Furthermore, your well-managed, spirited campaign may catch the eye of a power broker who can get you into the system as an appointee.

The Sacrificial Lamb: Many elected positions are held by politicians who, thanks to the powers of incumbency (read: money), have safe seats* they can never lose. Well aware of the fruitlessness of taking on such established electoral icons, most parties put up what's known as a "sacrificial lamb." If you find yourself in this position, don't despair. While you may get zero support from your party, political futures can change overnight and many an unknown strolled into office after the titans bit the dust.

Graceful Loser: Setting yourself up for a future election if you don't succeed the first time is a key reason not to be a sore loser. If you take the microphone on election night and lash out at your party, or the moronic voters, or your cheating, vote-buying opponent, you'll pretty much seal your own fate for the next time around. In addition, don't ruin the opportunity to stay relevant by establishing yourself as a "pundit" or "go to" person to discuss your opponent's performance and the issues of the day. Losing is not the end of the world, and everything you say and do should be geared toward the future. So be graceful and button the negative lip.

The process of lining up supporters and getting the nod is not a research project designed to help you make up your mind. Make a commitment and jump in. People will sense that you're half-hearted and waffling and will give you the same reaction. If you really want to run, run or go find something else to do.

Real Life Scenario: One of history's most famous losers who became a big winner is Abraham Lincoln. He lost bids for the Illinois state legislature, U.S. Senate, and vice president, but persevered to win a seat in Congress and was eventually elected president. Moral of the story: If you really want to be an elected official, don't give up–your turn will eventually come.

CAMPAIGN UPDATE

Mary was nervous as she prepared for a very important meeting. Carol was an acquaintance of William Kingsley, chairman of the Centerville Democratic Party, and they were going to talk to him about the race.

Mary did her research: the town council is made up of five elected officials—four council members and a supervisor—and they all serve two-year terms.

In Centerville, the supervisor is a Republican, as are two of the four council members. There are two Democrats. With three of the five town seats controlled by Republicans, they have the majority and pretty much control the town. If the Democrats pick up a seat, they would have the majority and the balance of power would shift. For this reason, Mary's race takes on greater importance.

Centerville has the ward system where each council member is elected to a specific district, while the supervisor runs "town wide." Mary would be up against Frank Amato, the Republican who represents the district where she lives.

"How much money do you have for the race?" was the first question out of Kingsley's mouth. Mary looked at Carol.

"Mr. Chairman," Carol spoke up. "I'm Mary's fundraiser and I'm confident we'll raise more than enough."

"Like how much?" Kingsley stayed focused on the green.

"Let me put it this way," Carol answered, "Milburn Pennybags has already committed the max, sixty-five-hundred, and we're lining up some other heavy hitters, as well as an aggressive campaign to raise money from smaller donors."

"Great," Kingsley said, seemingly impressed. He looked at Mary. "Why in the world do you want to run for town council?"

Mary anticipated the question and was ready with her Elevator Speech.

"I don't believe the taxpayers are getting a fair shake by the Republican majority," she told the chairman, making direct eye contact. "I've been to many town meetings where the cost-cutting initiatives and good government proposals from the Democrats go no-where. If we take back the town council, we can make some changes that will surely improve Centerville, im-press the voters and help build our Democratic base."

Kingsley nodded. Carol beamed.

"I've been a small business owner in this town for more than 25 years and I know a lot of people," Mary went on. "One thing I can tell you, Mr. Kingsley, is they're tired of what's going on at town hall and would welcome a fresh new face in our district. I'm that fresh new face."

"Well, there are a few other people interested in the race," Kingsley said, posing a non-committal stance.

"Mary just wants to go before the screening committee and get a fair shake, Bill," Carol interjected. "Our neighbor Joan Johnson's already on board. She's a member of the Democratic committee, isn't she?"

"A member of our executive board," Kingsley corrected her.

"Okay, then it's settled," Carol pushed. "Mary will appear before the screening committee."

"Okay. But I can't promise anything. We will have to let the process play out."

"Fair enough," Mary said reaching her hand to the chairman. "Thank you Mr. Kingsley. I look forward to working with you."

Mary and Carol repaired to the Centerville Diner.

"Here's a list of prominent Democrats I got from Joan," Carol dove right in. "Do you know anyone here?"

Mary scanned the list. "Look, here's Kevin Murray. I buy office equipment from him. He's the secretary of the party. And I know Gladys Rogers. I've been doing her taxes for years."

"Check off the ones you know and call them," Carol said. "I'll do the rest."

"What about the other two Democrats on the council?" Mary wondered.

"Call them right away and let them know what you're up to."

"I'll tell them we already met with Chairman Kingsley and I'm going to be screened."

"Brilliant!" Carol said. "Make it sound like you already have the chairman on your side. And don't forget to mention Joan."

Mary and Carol agreed to meet the following day to develop a list of other people and organizations that could support her race.

"Make sure we put the environmental groups on the list," Mary said. "They can't be too happy with Frank Amato's support of the mega mall."

The night of the screening Mary felt confident. She had made contact with some of the committee members and knew she would have some friendly faces in the room. She rehearsed her presentation so many times she could do it in her sleep.

"If our party doesn't back you, will you run a primary election against us?" Mary was asked before she could get out word one. She was prepared with a well-rehearsed speech and was going to announce her poll results to show she was the best candidate, and now her script was out the window.

It was a loaded question. If she said yes to a primary, the party would take offense and not view her as a team player. If she said no and they didn't pick her, she was out of the race unless she went against her word and ran a primary anyway.

"I believe I'm the best candidate for the position," Mary answered, "so I have confidence I'll be selected by my party."

"So you will run a primary if we don't pick you?"

"I don't know if I would. I'll have to make that decision when the time comes." Mary suddenly felt like the waffling politicians she so hated.

"We need to know now," the questioner pushed.

Mary's head spun through the options as every eye in the room stared her down.

"Yes. Yes I would run a primary," she finally answered.

The room looked annoyed.

For the rest of her presentation, Mary felt like a skater who fell on the first jump at the Olympics and lost her chance at gold.

Carol was livid. "I'm going to call Kingsley and tear him a new butt hole," she told the campaign team afterwards.

Rob, the Campaign Manager, sloughed it off. "It would be nice to get the party's endorsement, but if we have to wage a primary, then so be it. We'll win and take our momentum into the general election."

CHAPTER SEVEN

GETTING ON THE BALLOT

How do you actually run for office? What do you need to do to get on the ballot? What are the rules? The legalities? Suffice it to say, ignorance of the rules is not bliss—It will cost you.

Because of the money and power associated with elected office, lawyers are attracted to the process like sharks to a whale carcass. Winning an election by keeping your opponent off the ballot is a crafty way of coming out on top and some campaigns have gone all the way to the Supreme Court to win a race before a single vote is cast. An election won on a legal technicality is much easier than trusting it to the voters (and blowing a lot of money).

The Paperwork: Since most elections are parliamentary affairs, getting on the ballot requires paperwork and procedures. One slip up gives your opponents a free shot to knock you off and since these disputes usually end up in court, you'll need to make everything air tight.

Some states require petitions signed by voters registered to the party whose line the candidate is seeking. This is a grueling task designed to keep the major players with their petition-circulating minions and crafty election lawyers in power. They are just waiting for you to incorrectly word your paperwork or have someone sign your petition Jon Smith when their legal voting name is Jonathan. Know the rules in your area and follow them to a tee. Make sure your volunteers know the rules; give them an instruction sheet. Seek legal advice.

For every election campaign there's a lawyer or two looking to jump on the bandwagon.

Bonus: Send your petition signers a letter thanking them and stay in touch throughout the campaign; see if they'll volunteer.

Ballot Position: Your position on the ballot is another important consideration. Appearing as the first candidate the voters see is much better than being buried down the line. Most elections have rules pertaining to the ballot layout—some even draw straws to see who's on top. Find out how they do it in your particular race.

Bonus: Incorporate a copy of the ballot in your campaign literature so people know where to find you when they vote. Highlight your name in yellow. One candidate used her ballot position to her advantage: "Kim Johnson—The last name on the ballot, but first in the minds of the voters."

Beware: Treachery

Your "advisors" may be working both sides of the street and give you just enough wrong information so you slip up and then run to the other side to get credit for stifling your effort (don't roll your eyes, it happens).

June 1 is June 1 is June 1: If June 1 is the deadline for filing paperwork to run in your particular election, please note: June 2 is too late. There's nothing more disheartening than failing to get your required paperwork in on time. Miss the deadline and you are an instant loser.

Kick Them Off: And what the hay, why not scrutinize your opponents' paperwork and knock them off on a technicality? Always worth a shot and could save you a hell of a lot of time and effort.

Real Life Advice: Many times, the candidates themselves deliver the paperwork to make sure the deadline is met. And what about postmarks? If you mail your precious forms, do they have to arrive by June 1 or just be postmarked by June 1? Know the rules. Find out. And make sure you know of a 24-hour post office in your area.

Back Room Deals: Because controlling other people's money is such a lucrative occupation, don't think for one minute the bosses aren't divvying up the spoils in the back room. Sometimes, it's better for them to just maintain the status quo and when you thought your party was with you, the bosses have sold you down the river (and are in Bermuda while you're out there breaking your butt). Conversely, if the arrangement was to anoint you with only token opposition from the other side, would you take the deal?

Some elections involve runoffs where anyone can throw their hat in the ring. The top vote getters then face each other in the general election. Regardless of the seat you are seeking, there are specific rules and tactics to get on the ballot, so make sure you know the procedures so you get them right.

CAMPAIGN UPDATE Mary and Carol sat down with an acquaintance of Carol's, Henry Bratton, who's been involved in Centerville politics for years, for advice on getting on the ballot. He was very nice and laid out the entire process for them. Mary had to get the signatures of at least two percent of the voters registered to her party on a nominating petition, which in her case, was 200 Democrats. The petitions must be submitted to the Centerville Board of Elections by the close of business June 2, he told them.

"If you get the endorsement of the Democrat Party, they'll take care of the petition process and get you on the ballot," Bratton explained. "If not, and you still want to run, you can do your own petitions and force a primary election. Whoever wins will be the Democratic candidate in the general."

He said to come back if they needed the petition.

CHAPTER EIGHT

8 THE CAMPAIGN TEAM

Politics is a team sport and you absolutely can't do it alone. The very nature of the business–getting more people to vote for you than the other guy–mandates that you have people to help you get those votes.

The more important the office, the bigger the staff. The president and Congress control trillions of dollars. Therefore, their campaigns spend in the millions, with huge salaries going to staff and consultants. You may be able to get away with being a one-man band if you're running for an inconsequential seat, but anywhere in between, you're going to need some key personnel.

Bottom Line: Your staff can make or break you, so be sure to choose them well.

The Campaign Manager is the captain, the expert calling the shots, managing the staff, and making all the right decisions to get you elected. This is where the trouble starts. As the old saying goes, "The lawyer who represents himself has a fool for a client," and, sorry to say, the candidate is not the Campaign Manager.

We hear what you are thinking: *Well, it's my butt on the line, why shouldn't I call the shots?* You can have input and make suggestions and put your foot down when you feel strongly about something, but once you have your team and campaign game plan in place, you are infinitely better off campaigning than lording over every aspect of the race.

This assumes, of course, your staff knows what it's doing. There's nothing wrong with having long and detailed discussions with your team to make sure they have their act together, but once things get going, let them do their job. If you're running for an office of any consequence, you'll need to show you have some managerial skills, so why not start with your campaign staff?

Your Campaign Manager should be well versed in your narrative, platform and strategy—the concepts in this book—as well as the day-to-day game plan. They must know the roles of the other campaign staffers and should have the hours available to lead you to victory.

> A campaign is not managed by a "team." There has to be someone with clear authority to run the show, and that person is not the candidate. The team approach with everybody chiming in doesn't work because nothing gets done if everyone thinks they're in charge. Having a Campaign Manager who has the responsibility to act and is decisive—but may make a mistake or two—is better than one with no authority.

Beware: Chaos

Unless you're paying a professional, a capable volunteer Campaign Manager is hard to find. Whether you're relying on a friend or associate or someone sent by the party, you must spend some valuable time together to nail down exactly what you're going to do to win. Make the lines of communication crystal clear and visualize how things are going to work. Discuss the principles of this book. If it's not abundantly clear from the get-go how your team is going to perform, just wait until the heat of the campaign when your opponent starts throwing bombs.

The Other Half: This is a good time to contemplate another potential show stopper: The Spouse. Nothing riles a well-oiled machine more than having the significant other show up and start ordering people around. Sure, they have your best interest at heart, and nobody knows you like the better half, but unless your soul mate is a seasoned campaign pro, you must have a little talk with them—the sooner the better. In gentle but firm tones, have them understand that you appreciate all of their help and support and they can have a role in the campaign and can provide input like everyone else, but they're not the boss and must be able to work with the Campaign Manager and other staff. Do what you need to do to keep the Attila the Honeys from wreaking havoc on your well-laid plans.

If you decide to use your spouse in a major role, be careful with respect to their ability and commitment. You may want it more than they do and this will show when push comes to shove. You may find that your position on the issues and how to spend every waking moment during a heated election differs from your spouse's, who now occupies a key position in your operation, so proceed with caution!

Other problematic personalities, while we are on the subject, are the leaders and associates of the groups that are supporting you. They have magnanimously offered to throw their weight behind you and think they can call the shots. The situation gets even more dicey when they are paying for things like your advertising. No matter what direction you think the campaign should take, they are going to do it their way and possibly cost you the race. Worse yet, they will want to control the funds you have managed to raise. (This is all about money, remember?) Not a good position to be in, so understand it for what it is and do your best to move the decision making process toward your campaign's way of thinking and what's best for you.

Dwelling near the top of your campaign hierarchy can be a **Campaign Consultant.** This is a professional who's familiar with the ins and outs of running a campaign. The consultant should be able to digest the specifics of your race, help lay out the strategy and work with your team to get things done. They will monitor your progress and provide know-how and expertise. In the heat of battle when your opponent starts to hammer away at you, it's comforting to have a pro at your side guiding you over the bumps. Price of course plays a role in the quality of your consultants, so don't end up paying a little to get exactly that.

Campaign Treasurer: Another invaluable team member is the person you entrust with the money. A successful army may run on its stomach, but a campaign runs on money (read Chapter Three again). Without stringent management of your funds, your hands will be tied behind your back, and without a good Treasurer keeping things in order, you will run into trouble fast. Your Treasurer can be involved with raising money, but can also function as just the accountant with the checkbook.

Make sure your money handlers are well versed on The Rules. Taking in money can be a tricky business and if you make mistakes, you can lose the race or worse, find yourself with an indictment hanging over your head. In most races, there are limits on how much money you can accept from a person, business, or corporation. Every dime must be accounted for, including non-monetary donations (stamps, printing, vehicles, etc.). Many election laws require you to report every dollar going in and every dollar going out. Depending on what you are running for you may be required to make campaign filings with an elections board at various times during the race. Foul up the paperwork or blow a deadline and you are an easy target for your opponent: "If he can't even manage his own campaign, how could he possibly run our government?" It's the job of the Treasurer to keep you out of hot water.

Another thing your Treasurer must watch out for is the rouge donation from a questionable source. You could find yourself, as a mega mall opponent, explaining why your campaign accepted a $1,000 donation from the developer who wants to build the damned thing. Just ask losing presidential candidate Al Gore how much of a headache he had after taking money from a group of Buddhist monks.

The keeper of the purse strings must be an active part of the campaign and be readily available to disperse funds. Of course your Uncle Irving is the best accountant in the world and will watch your money like a hawk, but he may not know anything about election law. And try getting a check out of him for an emergency radio buy when your opponent just called you a Commie. Your campaign staff has more important things to do than chasing your Treasurer around for checks.

Fundraising Coordinator: Because of the importance of money in elections, it pays to have an active, hardworking, knowledgeable, skillful, (is that enough adjectives?) person raising your dough. The task is so important that some campaigns hire professionals and give them a cut of the proceeds. An ideal fundraiser knows a lot of people and is not afraid to shake the tree for your cause. They must also have the skills to manage fundraising events, direct mail appeals, and personnel for solicitation and follow up work.

Secretary/Scheduler: Who keeps track of all the crap going on in your life? However complicated your day-to-day existence was before you decided to run for office, it will get a lot more hectic during the campaign. As a candidate, you will be pushed and pulled in many directions. You have to show up on time. You have to appear to be on the ball. You have to deal with people who want something. If you are a dis-coordinated doofus during your campaign, your supporters—and the voters—will wonder just how effective you will be once in office. Your campaign Secretary/Scheduler (it can be the same person) should keep you straight.

During a heated race, a huge amount of minutiae will develop. Some of it may seem unimportant, but could sink you if not dealt with. Dates need to be confirmed, letters answered, your whereabouts known—all issues your Secretary should handle. While your Campaign Manager runs the campaign, your Secretary runs you. They must work together, remembering always that it all boils down to that fateful day when the voters go to the polls.

A critical function of your Secretary is developing your campaign schedule to get the most out of your fundraising activities and place you before the largest amount of voters. Should you go to the anti-mega mall rally or the Lion's Club meeting? What about the League of Women Voter's debate? Your Secretary needs to work this out with your Campaign Manager. Even if various events are on the same night, maybe you can attend them all if your Secretary plays your cards right. Your think-on-their-toes staff can let the Lions know you really want to see them, but you'll be about an hour late. As with most groups, this will probably be alright if you let them know in advance, and maybe even build a little anticipation.

An important adjunct to your Scheduling Secretary is your **Driver.** He/she is the one who gets you from point A to B on time and lets people know if are running late which, during a campaign, you will find yourself doing more often than not. People understand and it's alright–just call ahead! As noted in an earlier chapter, never show up alone. With a Driver, you'll have a built-in sidekick.

Real Life Scenario: Everyone at the mega mall rally will be voting for you. In fact, a big part of your candidacy is based on this issue. But miss the rally for whatever reason and not send your regrets or a stand in with an excellent reason for you not being there, then you'll lose them. They will stay home or vote for the other guy for the sole reason that you stood them up.

Hitting four or five events in one day is standard for a candidate. But which ones should be your priority? Again, your staff should work this out. Every place where there are people is a campaign stop—just don't miss the important ones. And if you do, communicate this well in advance or send a representative.

Office Manager: An easy way to get bad press is having a newspaper reporter drop in on your campaign headquarters and finding chaos or chirping crickets. This is where a good Office Manager is essential. They will need to keep the joint jumping and arrange things for the volunteers to do like stuffing envelopes or getting them on the phone to recruit their

Real Life Advice: Your Office Manager will want the HQ well stocked with not just office supplies, but beverages and snacks to keep the workers happy. A list of supplies to keep your nerve center humming is available in Chapter 14.

friends to stuff envelopes. The Office Manager will be there with the Secretary and they should complement one another. If there's not more than enough work for everyone then your campaign is not firing on all cylinders.

Spokesperson/Publicist: Once your platform is established and you are belting out your positions on the issues, who's going to communicate these gems to the public? Your publicist should have a grasp on the issues and know how to write a press release, position paper or speech. They should also have a familiarity with the local media and maybe even know some of the editors and reporters, if that's not asking too much. A necessity in our digital age is someone with Internet and Social Media skills to prepare your material for the widest distribution.

Real Life Scenario: Newspaper reporters make excellent publicists. They know how to write, how reporters think, and how to break down the issues so the average Joe can understand them. A local reporter will most likely have covered the office you are running for and know something about it.

Website/Social Media Manager: Internet use by candidates has exploded because it's a fast, cheap, and effective way to communicate with an ever-growing population of wired users. A dedicated staffer getting your messages out there through your website, Facebook page, tweets, LinkedIn, etc. will be worth their weight in gold, especially if they use this technology to promote your fundraising.

Volunteer Coordinator/Recruiter: Assigning a coordinator or even a team to find volunteers and put them to work for you is clutch. The more people spreading your message and turning out the vote the better, and if you have personnel dedicated to doing just that, you'll be well on your way. Since elections are a people business, you'll want people who know people, or at least a dedicated staff willing to convince people you don't know to come aboard.

Real Life Advice: As the candidate, make sure you treat your volunteers like the treasured resource they are. Spend time with them. Thank them and let them know how much their efforts mean to you. At the campaign headquarters, make sure they're never wanting for snacks or beverages. Order pizza and Chinese frequently and have a coffee maker with milk and half-and-half in the fridge. Your campaign budget should have a line item for keeping the troops happy.

Voter Registration Drive Coordinator: Since many elections go down to the wire, it pays to manufacture your own set of new voters. A registration drive, especially signing up voters under your party line, could add significantly to your tally. While they're at it, the coordinator can run down **absentee voters*—** people who can't make it to the polls, but can still cast a ballot for you.

Attorney: It's easier to win an election by knocking your opponent out of the race through legal maneuvers than it is to run a campaign. Therefore, at every step of the way, it's wise to have legal advice to make sure your i's are dotted and t's are crossed. Plus, if the tally is razor thin, there may be a legal battle over the legitimacy of your votes. Depending on your office, attorneys may work pro bono, which is for free, especially if you're running under a party label that has legal services at its disposal. In any case, your attorney should give you a break on their fee since making a connection to an office holder is a plus for those in the legal field.

Researcher: What's your opponent's position on the issues? Have they ever said something to the contrary? What are the hot topics of the day? What are the papers writing about? A Researcher can mine the Internet, meeting minutes, old clippings, Social Media, etc. to uncover valuable Intel and keep tabs on what's going on. Even before the campaign gets underway, knowing the issues at hand and what skeletons your opponent has in the closet is a blessing.

Coordination With Other Campaigns: Another key operation of your staff is coordinating activities with your running mates. Maybe you want to show up to an event as a team or knock on doors together. Or, how about sending out a team mailing instead of a solo affair? Raising money as a team also works well, especially if you are lesser known than your running mates. And make sure you don't schedule your fundraiser the same time as theirs.

Changing Staff Members: In some races, changes to your staffing situation can be breaking news, especially if you have to fire someone or they storm off in a huff. Your best defense is carefully considering who you take on in the first place. Remember, in the money-driven, weasel-world of politics, everyone is out for themselves. So if your high-priced consultant or the power broker's nephew wants to score points at your expense, they can always storm out of your campaign, hold a press conference on why you're a loser, and take their knowledge to the other side. This can take on Faustian proportions when their incompetence is what put your campaign behind the eight ball in the first place.

So, what do you do with the bad apple? If you fire them, they run to the other side (which will be more than happy to take them in). Or if it gets so bad they have no choice but to quit, think about it—What's their best option? You guessed it, run to your competitor. The antidote, we cannot stress enough, is to assemble your team carefully from the get go and run a professionally managed campaign.

Beware: Spies

In many elections, there may be so much at stake (read: money), that it pays to employ spies, double agents, etc. It hurts to send out a campaign pitch only to have it shot down by your opponent before it even reaches the voters' mailboxes. While the following point may be a question of too little too late, we include it for educational purposes. It's easy to figure out who the spies are after the election: They're the ones who (or their family members) get hired—or keep their jobs—under your opponent.

Sign Patrol: An effective marketing tactic is the proper placement of signs, posters, and bill boards. Name recognition means just that—people seeing your face and knowing your name. The Sign Patrol should organize all placements, including delivering signs, posters, bumper stickers, etc. to whoever can put them up. They'll work out logistics such as ordering, locations and getting permission. Having supporters put lawn signs on their property or posters in their stores or offices shows you have people behind you and exposes your name to the electorate.

Make sure your volunteers know not to put up signs willy-nilly. Don't put them on public property and private locations where you don't have permission or it will become a campaign issue. Don't wallpaper stop signs with bumper stickers and don't nail signs to trees. No matter how tempting, don't get caught taking down your opponent's signs.

Real Life Scenario: If your office is of any consequence, you'll probably be able to hire some staff once you are elected. These positions can be well-paid and may very well confer some power and authority to your chief of staff, office manager, etc. Watch Out! Competition for these jobs will start on the campaign trail and the more devious members of your team will try to box out everyone else for the plum positions. This kind of turmoil is an unnecessary distraction and could very well sink your effort.

CAMPAIGN UPDATE

Mary grabbed a legal pad and sat down with Carol to talk about who they could get to join the campaign team. They already had Bernard as the Website/Social Media guy and Mary brought up name of her Uncle Saul for Treasurer.

"Does Saul have an office nearby?" Carol wanted to know to make sure he would be available to cut checks as needed.

"He does," Mary answered, "and not only that, he has a friend who's been the Treasurer for a few campaigns he can work with to make sure we cover all the rules."

"Excellent," Carol said. "You're going to make a great councilwoman." Then she took on an expression of concern: "What about Tom? How does he feel about all this?"

"He's okay. I know he wants to help, but I just don't know what to do with him."

"Once we get a little more organized, let's sit down with him and see what he wants to do," Carol said. "I just want to make sure he's comfortable with his role and is able to help."

"Totally agree. The last thing we need is a prima donna getting in our hair," Mary said as the two ladies laughed.

"What about a Campaign Manager?"

"You know what? Bernard knows a nice young man who was the president of the college Democrats. He has a degree in political science and was involved in a few of the state races," Carol said. "Let's interview him. Or, we could put some feelers out to hire a professional."

"Before we interview anyone, I want to be clear on what we're looking for and how this race should be managed," Mary said. She went over the following:

- The Campaign Manager should have experience and an open mind about learning what they don't know (like what's in this book).
- They should be able to work with us to create a campaign strategy with a direct mail plan, advertising, budget, Get-Out-The-Vote effort, and other essentials.
- They should have a grasp on the issues and be able to relate them to the campaign.
- They should be organized and willing to follow an agenda.
- They should work well with others and be able to manage people.

"I don't think Bill Clinton's available, but we'll see what we can do," Carol joked.

"Betty from my office will be my Secretary and a few doors down, a space opened up where we can have our headquarters for pretty cheap—I know the landlord. I already have Betty working on the lease and some office equipment, phones, supplies. She keeps my schedule as it is and she's very organized. I'm going to let her work over there as the Office Manager as well. I think she'll do great."

"Do you think we should look for a paid consultant?" Carol asked.

"We're doing okay so far, so let's hold off on that one. What about a media person?"

"I like Linda Smith. She used to work for the Centerville Post. Let's sit down with her," Carol said.

"Great. Put a check mark next to that one."

"Guess what? I ran into Lou Rosso. He's retired from the school and spends most of his time in the library reading newspapers and talking to people. Are you thinking what I'm thinking?"

"Perfect! He'd make a great Research guy. Can you talk to him?"

"Check."

"Next is a volunteer person. I need all the help I can get."

"What about the Rotary Club? You've been a member for years. Isn't there anyone there who can help?"

Mary's eyes lit up. "Max Baumgartner, the president! We've known each other for a long time. He would be perfect."

"Check, check, and check!"

"Okay. I think we got our work cut out for us staffing this thing," Mary said. "Let's keep asking around. I'll need a Driver, Sign patrol, lawyer. Let's get to work!"

"Amen."

SPECIAL SECTION:
Your First Campaign Meeting

The first session with your assembled team, advisors, and various arm-chair quarterbacks will be an interesting experience. Everyone will be chiming in with words of wisdom and it could go on forever.

The best way to stay on track is to create an agenda and stick to it. Let everyone get in their two cents worth, but make sure all of the critical campaign items are covered in an orderly manner. The Campaign Manager should run the meeting, but the candidate sets the tone and should weigh in when things get out of hand. Make it crystal clear what is expected of everyone. Stress the need for professionalism and the importance of sticking to the game plan. To avoid an all-nighter, nudge the conversation back on point when necessary.

Have the Secretary keep a running agenda. Add to it as the campaign unfolds and use it to make sure everyone is doing what they're supposed to. This is a vital managerial process that will serve you well once you get elected—and especially if you go for a higher office.

Campaign meetings have a tendency to devolve into opinion sessions on what you should and shouldn't do. Using the agenda as a checklist from meeting to meeting, you will be able to differentiate between those who perform and those who like to tell everyone else what to do.

Be wary of the characters who have years of campaign "experience," but in reality, just like to hear themselves talk. They'll monopolize your time and turn off those who really have something worthwhile to say.

Hear everyone out and don't let overbearing personalities drown out discussion. In the end, make decisions and get going.

A winning campaign assigns jobs to those with the ability to get things done and supports them as they progress. This is why it's critical to have a Campaign Manager acting as a taskmaster to set goals, provide necessary tools and guidance, and follow up as necessary to make sure the effort is moving forward.

Real Life Scenario: One of the more bizarre—and time consuming—meeting topics, you'll see, is the discussion about campaign colors. Everyone has an opinion. What color should the bumper stickers be? The signs? What are the best colors for a campaign? Red, white, and blue always work. Whatever you choose, be consistent between signs, bumper stickers, website, etc. so people can identify you by your colors. Don't use yellow for one thing, and green for another—that'll just confuse people. If you're running against the mega mall, green is a good environmental color. Your printer should have a feel for it. Also, stay with the colors of your team. If the head of your ticket is using red and blue, don't go lime green. If your party has been using red, white and blue for the last 10 elections and they have been winning, don't come out of the box with brown and gold. On the other hand, if your party has been losing, maybe some new colors with your fresh face are in order. Companies that sell campaign items have some great examples online—check them out.

CAMPAIGN UPDATE

Mary called her first campaign team meeting and opened by thanking everyone and sharing her thoughts on why she's running and how she plans to win. She introduced the key players to each other and thought to herself, *So far, so good.*

Mary and Carol interviewed a half dozen people to manage the campaign and were most impressed by the former college Democrat president, Rob Carter, who demonstrated some campaign knowledge and a wealth of enthusiasm. He was introduced to Bernard, the Website/Social Media Manager and Uncle Saul, the Treasurer. Also on board were Max Baumgartner, the Rotary president who agreed to be Mary's Volunteer Coordinator, Spokesperson/Publicist Linda Smith, Betty the Secretary/Scheduler and Office Manager, and Lou Rosso, Researcher.

Mary turned the meeting over to Rob who passed out an agenda.

"Thank you Betty for agreeing to take notes and keeping the agenda up to date," Rob opened with. "Betty is also Mary's Scheduler and was kind enough to post a campaign calendar online," Rob continued. He handed out a sheet with the log-in information to access the calendar in Google Docs. "Check with me or Betty if you want anything added to the schedule."

The first item on the agenda was money.

"Carol, can you give us a report on the fundraising side?" Rob asked.

Carol wheeled off a list of six fundraisers she was planning as well as two direct mail appeals.

"Bernard, can you coordinate with Carol as far as posting the events on the website and a Social Media campaign?" Rob followed up.

"Already on it. We set up an online ticket purchase system through eBrite and have the first event on Facebook. Mary's got a pretty good following already with 230 Facebook likes and 730 email addresses in her data base. Her blog about last Tuesday's town council meeting got 450 hits."

"Wow," Rob said, "and we haven't even officially announced her candidacy yet."

"Let's get to that," Mary jumped in, but was quick to apologize for interrupting. "I'm being screened by the Democrats on Thursday. Should I announce my candidacy before that or should we wait?"

"Let's not wait," Rob replied. "Let's get it out to the world before the screening, let those Democrats know we're serious. Linda, can you put together a release?" (See Linda's work at the end of the update.)

"Absolutely, and I think we should go see my old boss at the Centerville Post. I know he'd like the system shaken up a little bit and will appreciate Mary's energy."

"What's the best way to get the word out?" Mary asked.

"I have a list of all the media outlets and already put together a press kit. I think we should do a press conference right on the steps of town hall."

Everyone looked at Mary.

"Outstanding. Count me in!"

After the meeting, Rob sat privately with the candidate. "I'm not being nosy, but I want to ask you if there is anything in your background we should know about in case it comes up in the campaign."

"No, nothing. I'm just a local businesswoman, happily married."

"You weren't a member of the Weather Underground? Been arrested? Anything like that?"

"Nope, nothing to worry about."

"Great, and by the way," Rob finished, "I'm glad everyone likes the campaign colors: red, white and blue."

LOCAL BUSINESSWOMAN ANNOUNCES CAMPAIGN FOR TOWN COUNCIL
MARY MORGAN TARGETS HIGH TAXES AND WASTEFUL SPENDING

For Immediate Release.........................…..May 30, 2014
Contact Linda Smith...........................…..653-555-1234

Mary Morgan, a Centerville businesswoman for more than 25 years, has announced her candidacy for the town council on a platform of cutting high taxes and wasteful spending.

Morgan, a life-long Centerville resident, is a leader in the fight against the Carson mega mall and has a long history of community involvement. She is a two-decade volunteer with the Centerville Rotary serving as president and member of the board of directors, and a past president of the Friends of the Library.

"I believe I share the view of many Centerville residents that taxes are too high and the current town council isn't doing enough to strengthen our economy and create jobs," Morgan said in announcing her run for the 3rd District on the steps of town hall. "Senior citizens can no longer afford to live here and our younger people are leaving in droves because they can't find work."

Morgan said she is preparing a multi-faceted economic plan for Centerville and looks forward to spotlighting key local issues such as town hall spending, better services, and efforts to bolster the downtown business district.

"There's been a shortage of ideas and initiatives coming out of town hall to put Centerville back on track and I intend to change

continued

that," Morgan said.

A married mother of three who operates a successful financial planning firm on Main Street, Morgan will be seeking the Democratic nomination for the seat.

###

CHAPTER NINE
GETTING YOUR MESSAGE TO THE VOTERS

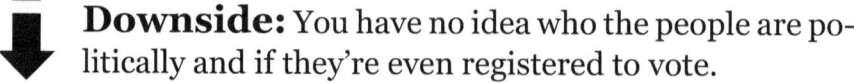

Since the days of orating from the back of a railroad car are gone, most races require that you mass communicate. In this chapter, we will cover all of the ways you can reach the voters, starting from the most basic to the most technologically advanced.

In a nut shell, the goal is to connect with the greatest amount of voters as frequently as you can. Let's work our way through 11 ways to do it:

#1 Random Face-to-Face: Showing up at train stations, country fairs, and community events and introducing yourself to the people you encounter is as basic as campaigning gets.

Upside: It's free, upfront, and personal.
Downside: You have no idea who the people are politically and if they're even registered to vote.

#2 Organized Events: An effective way to meet people one-on-one is at events you create or where you are an invited guest. You'll get more traction mingling with people at the mega mall rally than with commuters waiting for the train, and you can be assured of some friendly faces in the crowd. As an invited guest at the Elks club, you will have the imprimatur of whomever invited you. Your supporters can organize a coffee klatch in their homes or a meet the candidate night. If you have the endorsement of an established organization, be part of their events. The key is to speak before large, friendly crowds that you have a connection to.

 Upside: You'll have a chance to nail down voters already inclined to support you.

Downside: It takes effort and organization to assemble the biggest crowds possible.

Preaching to the Choir: Groups you belong to will naturally vote for you. If you're a life-long member of the Presbyterian Church, you can expect the parishioners to go your way. That is if you don't take them for granted. One easy way to sour a natural voting bloc is to stop going to their meetings because you are too busy courting others. Make sure you solidify your base and then expand outwards to groups you have to work a little harder to win over. Obviously, you should avoid groups that are diametrically opposed to you. If you are a Democrat, there's probably no need to go to the Young Republican meeting, unless maybe there's a hook–your nephew is a member and has invited you. Your staff can determine if it's worth your time.

Tips on Working the Crowd:

- Going it alone makes it look like you have no supporters, so make sure you show up with an entourage, preferably with some members of the group you are visiting.

- Go in with the goal of making direct contact with everyone there. Be friendly and smile—shake hands, hug babies, have your picture taken. If you see someone you know, carry on like you're life-long friends; slap some backs.

- Do some research and be ready to talk about issues germane to the crowd. Weave their issues into your discussions.

- Listen intently to what the people are telling you. Let them talk.

- Carry a note pad and take down contact information. Make people think you care (and don't forget to follow up).

- Be ready to quickly and briefly handle the softball—Q: "So, Mary, why do you want to be our next town councilwoman?" A: "Lisa, I think we can do a better at town hall lowering taxes and bringing more jobs to the area. With your help, I'm confident we can make a difference. Can I get your email address so we can stay in touch?"

- Move Along—Lisa will want to tie you up in a 20-minute discourse, so practice the art of moving along. Have your wing man move you from voter to voter and rescue you from the long-winded types that will keep you from meeting more people. Your lead person can also help you collect contact information to build your data base and keep track of people you need to get back to.

- Give out pens, combs, nail files, or little note pads with your name on them. Leave them with a...

#3 Palm Card or Brochure: This is your primary outreach tool, what the voters will peruse to find out more about you and make their decision on who to vote for. Make it glossy with the highest quality paper and printing you can afford.

Adorn it with a flattering picture or two and make your case as to why people should vote for you. Put them in as many hands as you can; pretend each one is a vote. Go to **www.WinAnElection.org** for some great examples.

 **Upside:** Proven campaign tool, gets your message directly to the voters.
Downside: Production costs, making sure your wording and layout are effective.

There's one key word when it comes to your campaign literature: **Brevity**. No one will wade through a bunch of verbiage to figure out what you're trying to say. Once you decide on the points you want to get across, boil them down to the least amount of words. Create a bulleted list with three or more related items and make them bold for emphasis. Mary Morgan will:

- *Fight* **to reduce taxes**
- *Battle* **government spending**
- *Work* **to provide better services**

Note the action words: ***Fight, Battle, Work.***

Artistry/Design: Once you have the words down pat, don't drop the ball on the "look" of your work. Your designer should lay out a compelling piece with your logo, campaign colors, photos, bulleted lists with bold letters and italics for emphasis, and other features to give your material a professional look with pizzazz—something voters will want to read. Pictures allow you to connect with people on an emotional level. Photos of you with babies and grandmas will help you connect better than just a bunch of words.

Real Life Scenario: When Brookhaven Town Supervisor Ed Romaine campaigns at sidewalk fairs, he gives out shopping bags with his bumper stickers stuck on the outside and his handouts inside. As the recipients make their way through the vendors, they'll put their purchases in his bags and then take them home.

Bonus: Get your picture taken with people you meet like the one Romaine got with a lady on her bike with his bag in the front basket. These look great in your campaign material and Social Media posts.

#4 Door Knocking: A potent campaign technique is going to the homes of enrolled voters and meeting them face to face. Knock on the door and unleash your Elevator Speech. You'll get various reactions, but overall, people will be amazed that you actually took the time to come see them. Let them talk. If they have a problem, promise to look into it and make a note. Ask them flat out if you can have their vote. Go with one or two other people so you don't look like a loner and leave your palm card or brochure.

⬆ **Upside:** Visiting people on their home turf is very powerful, especially if you follow up. These are the people you want to drive to the polls.

⬇ **Downside:** Going door to door is hard work and time consuming. Some candidates wear out shoes, some give up after a day or two.

Unless they run you off the property, keep track of everyone you meet. Send them a follow up note about how glad you were to meet them (and remind them to vote). Send them more mail, and the week before the election, make sure they are contacted again. Have your **Get Out The Vote (GOTV)** team target them specifically since a huge percentage of the people you contact this way will vote for you.

Avoid having someone drive you from house to house. That just comes off as lazy, unless the voters you are visiting live far apart or you have a good reason for not being able to walk. Hit the doorbell and then knock. Give people time to answer. Also, remove your sunglasses so you can look them square in the eye when you introduce yourself.

> **Bonus:** If no one's home leave a "Sorry I missed you" card. The ones that have a hook to go over the door knob are pretty effective.

#5 If you can't go door-to-door, **Hit the Phones.** Same principles apply: Call people and give them your speech. If they want to yak, let them yak and don't hang up without a commitment. If they're not with you, make a note of it. If they are, make sure they vote.

Upside: Easier and faster than knocking on doors.

Downside: Not as personal as face-to-face and some people don't like to be aggravated by phone calls.

Phone Banks: You can only make so many phone calls as a solo act, but dozens of supporters can make many. Provide your phone callers with well-written scripts and give them a lesson on phone skills. Have them practice with the staff a few times before you unleash them on the world. (See the scripts later in this chapter.)

Upside: You can rack up an impressive volume of human-to-human contact.

Downside: Organizing phone banks and staffing them with volunteers who know what they're doing can be a wearisome logistical exercise that requires advance planning and hands-on management. Plus, some people don't like to be aggravated by phone calls.

> **Real Life Scenario:** Putting together the walk and call lists is a vital political science. A detailed analysis of where you can expect your votes to come from so you can go after them is critical to your success. Breaking down the electorate into manageable groups is discussed in detail in Chapter Eleven, Building a Winning Majority, so for now, let's just stay with the ways you can make your connections.

Vital to a successful phone campaign is the list of names and numbers your callers will use. While it's tempting to contact every voter to get them to see the light, its best to focus on your base—members of your party or the organizations that support you. Don't take your natural constituencies for granted. If you are running as a Democrat, call the Democrats.

> **Real Life Advice:** Your call list may boil down to volunteers looking up numbers. Your board of elections or other authority can provide names and addresses of voters and maybe even phone numbers. There are also companies that provide lists and getting the right ones is well worth the expense.

Make sure they hear from you. Make sure they vote.

Systems are available to enable your supporters to call voters from anywhere using a computer, laptop, or smart phone (make sure they have an unlimited calling plan). Callers log on and the system displays a script, voter's name, and dials the number. If someone answers, the caller is off and running. If an answering machine picks up, the system will leave your powerful message and the caller can go on to the next one without waiting. The system lets the caller log in results and makes it easy to place thousands of live calls.

There are also commercial call centers that will handle your entire calling operation, including assembling lists, making calls, and logging voter response.

While a computerized system makes phone calling easy, you can still do it with good, old fashioned paper lists. Just make sure you have some very organized people keeping track of what everyone is doing.

Beware: Do Not Call

Some people are on the Do Not Call Registry and may get p.o.'ed if you call them. The registry doesn't apply to political candidates, so a simple "Sorry to bother you" will get you off the phone without much harm done.

Campaigns live and breathe by two phrases: **Voter ID and GOTV.** Your first round of phoning can find out if the voter is leaning toward you or your opponent—Voter Identification—and the next can Get Out The Vote from those who said they favor you. The following two scripts sum it up:

Phone Script #1—Voter ID:

Hello Mr. Jones? My name is Carol and I'm calling about the upcoming town election. Do you mind if I ask you real quick (before they have a chance to say yes or no): *Are you leaning toward voting for Mary Morgan for the town council or Frank Amato? Mary Morgan—great. Don't forget to vote on November 4. And do you think you can do us one more favor? Remind your family and friends to vote for Mary as well. It's very important. Thank you.*

If they say they're with Amato, thank them and go on to the next call.

The caller logs the answers and now you have a data base of people who said they will vote for you. Next step: Make sure these people vote.

Phone Script #2—GOTV:

Hello Mr. Jones? My name is Carol and I'm calling about the election on Tuesday. Are you definitely going to vote? Great. Can I ask you one quick favor? Don't forget to vote for Mary Morgan for the town council and please remind your family and friends to vote as well. This is a very important position and we know Mary will do a great job. You won't forget will you? Thank you. We really appreciate it.

It goes without saying, but there's no need to call back the people who said they were with the other guy.

Robo Calls: It's fairly easy to set up an automatic calling system—you can buy a program for your computer—or you can hire a company to set it up for you (Google "robo calls"). The recorded voice can be yours with an important message for the voters or a familiar name in the community, maybe a trusted elected official or even a celebrity.

For example, you've run into Congressman Poplar a few times on the campaign trail and he's offered to help. He's been around for ages and has brought home millions to the district. A robo call from him would go something like this:

This is Congressman Poplar calling about a very important vote coming up. Mary Morgan is running for the Centerville Town Council and I would consider it a personal favor if you cast your ballot for her.

Mary will watch our tax dollars and help make sure our town remains a great place to live, work, and raise a family. I've spent my career urging people to take their right to vote seriously and this Tuesday, I want you to exercise your right. Please vote for Mary Morgan. Thank you.

When people visit your website, lo and behold there's an audio of the Congressman's announcement with a picture of you and him. It's also on Facebook and YouTube and it's racking up hits.

#6 Meet the Candidates Night: Your path will inevitably cross your opponent's and Meet the Candidates will be one of the likely places. When you get there, follow the tips on working the crowd and be cordial to the other side. You will have an opportunity to give your Platform Speech and then get questions from the audience. Your research will prepare you for the type of questions you'll get. If you're on the stage with your opponent and you're answering the same questions, it may be a good time to point out your differences and why people should vote for you instead. Be prepared to have some shots taken at you and throw in some digs yourself. (Please read further on about the dreaded Foot-in-Mouth Disease).

 Upside: You can make your case for election in front of an interested group.

 Downside: Your opponent has the same opportunity.

While You're There: In addition to meeting voters and stating your case, there are a few important things you should take away from these get-togethers:

- Note the issues people bring up and take a position on them. Work them into a mailing specific to the group; offer solutions to their problems and promise to fight for them.

- Recruit people to your campaign team, particularly the president or the officers; get your picture taken with them. See if they'll do a mailing for you or give you their membership list.

- Ask if the group will make an endorsement or conduct a straw poll to see where the membership stands. If they endorse you, run with it—hard.

- Make an important announcement you know the group will appreciate; have your staff hand out a press release.

- If there are reporters there, make sure they get your side of the story. Get interviewed; smile for the camera!

- Have everything videotaped and use your better quips for your advertising and Internet posts. Maybe you'll get footage of your opponents saying something stupid.

At the end, while the crowd is still milling about, shoot a quick video and post it on your website, Facebook page, and YouTube. Pull in a few supporters from the audience and capture some positive feedback from them.

> *"This is Mary Morgan, candidate for the Centerville Town Council, live from a meeting with the League of Woman Voters. There are many here who appreciate my plans to cut taxes and make local government more responsive to the people..."*

Shortly after, send the president and board a thank you; ask that they share it with the membership. Send out a press release about you being there and the issues that were discussed (and your commitment to resolving them); include a photo of you with the group.

#7: A beefier version of meet the candidates, is the **debate** where you can go at it head to head with the other side. Again, preparation is key. Anticipate the questions you'll be asked and practice your answers. If the event is sponsored by the VFW, be ready with your views on veteran's issues. If you're in a high tax area, detail your economic plan—How will you lower taxes? Which government services will you cut? Why, when you served on the library board, did the library tax go up? Research your opponent and be ready to hammer away at why he raised taxes, or supported the mega mall or whatever the issues of the day are.

 Upside: You can draw distinctions between you and your opponents and challenge their views.

 Downside: Your opponent can do the same. Is a draw the best you can hope for?

It also pays to salt the audience with friendly faces and, if possible, have them serve up softball questions to you (and make it hard on your opponents). It's comforting to have louder applause and a more enthusiastic audience than your rivals.

Rule of 10: If you memorize and clearly deliver 10 topics pertinent to your campaign, you will come off as a genius. Imagine if you were at a cocktail party and each guest had at least 10 interesting things to say, it probably wouldn't be so boring.

On the campaign trail, you must be both entertaining and able to convince people to support you. Just as important, you must constantly be on guard against saying the wrong thing. A master politician will take any question, any line of thought or debate and deftly turn it back to one of their 10 points.

Real Life Scenario: Missouri Senator Claire McCaskill successfully defended her seat against Congressman Todd Akin, who was leading in the polls until he uttered the following: "If it's a legitimate rape, the female body has ways to try to shut that whole thing down." Yikes!

Real Life Scenario: "I'm not going to prosecute every man who belts his wife across the face," was the infamous quote uttered by Suffolk District Attorney candidate Jim Catterson when asked about his position on domestic violence. This wasn't an issue he thought about or a key point he wanted to get across to the voters, just a knee-jerk remark that almost sank his campaign (and pretty much did when he sought reelection).

There are two classic ways your mouth can get you in trouble. **The first** is when you speak extemporaneously, off the cuff. Don't go outside of the script and comment on something you're not prepared for. If it's not something you've thought about previously, don't wing it. There's nothing wrong with saying, "I don't know" or "I'll have to get back to you on that."

The second way to suffer a self-inflicted wound is by trying to score points at the expense of someone else, usually in the form of an off-color joke or comment. Racial and offensive humor will get you in hot water faster than someone can hit "send" on their smart phone. Never, ever poke fun at or reference someone's race, color, religion, origin, relatives, handicap, clothes, hair, beliefs, creed, background, history, family, illness, etc.—it's all off limits. If you're with a group that hates another group and you're tempted to make a crack, don't do it. Propping yourself up by cutting someone else down is strictly verboten.

The Moral of the Story: Never, ever say anything publically or in a private setting you haven't hashed out, rehearsed, and run by your brain trust as something you want the world to know. Off-hand remarks are a reflection of the true you and they're what the people really want instead of safe, canned lines. Be yourself and speak freely, just make sure you stick to the script and not let slip with something you'll regret.

**Beware:
It's Never Private**

Always assume that you're being recorded. Your inappropriate remarks will still be devastating even if you think you're making them privately. Ask Mitt Romney how he got hammered when the mic caught him saying: "There are 47 percent of the people who will vote for the president no matter what, who are dependent upon government, who believe that they are victims. These are people who pay no income tax, and so my job is not to worry about those people." Guess how many of those people voted for him?

#8 Media Coverage: Your race will most likely be of interest to the Fourth Estate (a highfalutin name for the local press) and it's a good idea to seek out the reporters who will be covering the race, as well as their bosses, the editors. Earned media,* as it's called, is free, but you still have to work for it. News stories will connect you to audiences you would otherwise have to spend a lot of money to reach. To facilitate the coverage, you will want to provide a...

Press Kit containing the following:

- Photograph you wouldn't be embarrassed to see on the cover of People Magazine.
- Your narrative summing up who you are, background, experience, activities, endorsements, why you are running, what you aim to accomplish, etc. You can also include your resume.
- Platform explaining, briefly, where you stand on the issues.
- Palm card or brochure.

Create digital versions of your material you can email and burn to a CD in a form that can be easily opened such as a Word doc or PDF. Some reporters are lazy and many times will use what you give them verbatim, so make it easy to cut and paste. Put your press material in a nice folder (not neon orange) and make it a point to deliver one to each and every reporter and editor covering your area. Ask to set up an...

Editorial Interview: If you're serious about running for a particular office, read what's been written about that office, the incumbents, and how the editors feel about what's going on. If it's an important race, they'll want to meet you and possibly make an endorsement (it doesn't hurt to advertise in these papers either). Expect to provide more specifics than your usual stump speech and prepare for harder questions than the meet the candidates night. This is your chance to make a compelling case to people who are going to tell your story to potentially thousands and thousands of readers and maybe even endorse you in the process.

Endorsements and editorial interviews are not just limited to print media: television, radio, and even Internet bloggers and online newspapers can expose you to thousands. Reach out to these sources and try to generate some coverage. A story about the race, an interview, or a feature about you would be great to reproduce, post, tweet and link to from your website.

 Upside: The media allows you to reach large audiences for free.

Downside: You can't control what they write, so if they're against you, the coverage can be pretty brutal, especially if they latch onto something juicy.

The Written Word: A big part of your campaign—press releases, brochures, speeches, position papers, posts, blogs, comments, etc.—will rely on the written word. Your advisors will all have expert opinions on what you should say, but it's just hot air until someone sits down and actually writes the thing. Good writers, especially those with campaign experience, are a huge asset. They can absorb all the input and produce a draft. Once you have a document you can work with, start the fine-tuning process and produce something you can be proud of.

What you put out there can make or break your campaign, so make sure it's well written. Here are some tips:

Your Voice: Does your material sound like it's coming from you, in your voice? How does it sound when you read it out loud? Does it flow? Does it make sense? Think about how people will perceive it. Does it get your message across? Does it make your salient points? Make sure your words sound like they're coming from you and not Winston Churchill.

Beware: The Truth Always Be Told

Campaign lore is littered with candidates who lied about their credentials and got torched. Whatever you say or put down on paper will be scrutinized, so don't fudge the facts. If you attended Harvard, but didn't graduate, don't say you're a Harvard grad. Likewise, if you were stationed in Missouri during Operation Desert Storm, don't say you served in the Gulf. While we're on the subject of honesty, don't plagiarize other people's words because here's what will happen: Someone will do a Google search on your gems of wisdom and if they come back as written by someone else, you're toast.

Quotes: A good way to nail home a point is stating it in some-one's own words. By the third or fourth paragraph of a press release, for example, quote somebody, or yourself. If you are writing about jobs, put in a quote from a local businessperson. If you're focusing on high taxes, cite a family that's having trouble making ends meet. Quotes go beyond the dry facts of your material and provide the color commentary.

Typos and Run-Ons: Word processors have spell checks and even grammar checks—use them. Send something out to the world with misspelled words and run-on sentences and your credibility will go down the drain. Always have someone look over your stuff one last time before it goes out; read it to others.

Double check facts, names, places, numbers, quotes (make sure they're opened and closed), etc. Once you put it out there, it's official and if it's wrong, you open yourself up to ridicule.

> **Bonus:** Set up a photo shoot to make sure you have enough pictures for your brochures, ads, etc. Line up kids and sen-iors; choose a few different locations. Show yourself in ac-tion—shaking hands, listening intently. See if VIPs and rep-resentatives of the groups supporting you will pose.

Press releases should be done in a newspaper style like an article you'd see in the paper. Reporters and editors are always under the gun and don't have time for rewrites. The more your release sounds like something you'd see in their paper, the more likely they are to run it the way you wrote it. Use the **"inverted pyramid"** style, that is, put the most important stuff in the beginning and items of lesser importance toward the end, and don't forget a headline.

The Press Conference: A great way to reach the media and stimulate coverage is a press conference. The reasons you might call out the press are varied and limited only by your imagination. Indeed, wily politicians and PR pros come up with some real doozies to generate stories. The media isn't there to serve as your communications department, so make it worth their while. Your relationship with the press—being straight with them and giving them newsworthy items—will go a long way toward attracting them to your events. Here are but a few things you can do to spark their interest:

- Announce a new idea or initiative
- Respond to a current event
- Highlight a new aspect of your campaign
- Trot out a major endorsement
- Criticize your opponent
- Answer criticism
- Help someone with a cause
- Release statistics
- Report a victory
- Disclose legal action

A well-executed press conference starts with picking an appropriate **location** such as the steps of town hall or a place associated with your topic. If you're announcing something about your campaign, do it at your headquarters. A current event? Go to where the event occurred. If you're getting endorsed by the anti-mega mall crowd, go to the site. If you want to challenge your opponents, go to their headquarters.

If you're indoors, make sure you have proper seating and don't pick a cavernous hall so you look like an ant. Know where the outlets are so the reporters can plug in. If you're outdoors, pick a rain date and be ready to notify everyone if you have to call it off. Make sure you can be heard—line up a PA system or megaphone. Have your staff visit the site ahead of time for a run through. Is there adequate parking?

Pick an appropriate **time.** If you want to be on the six o'clock news, don't do it at 5:30 and if your main weekly newspaper comes out on Wednesdays, don't do it Tuesday afternoon. Weekends are a slow news cycle, so avoid Fridays (unless you have something bad you need to get out there). The Fourth Estate's usually hustling on Monday, so cut them some slack. No reporter wants to get up at the crack of dawn or stay out late, so pick a reasonable hour—late morning gives them time to file their report. Also, they don't want to travel to the middle of nowhere, so make the location as convenient as you can.

Make sure you're on time.

The event will be a **theatrical presentation** so have a nice backdrop, podium, and plenty of supporters, including the people associated with your issue. For visual impact, have them hold signs and fill in behind you to make it look like you have a sea of support. These images will be perfect for your press release, campaign literature, website, Social Media, etc.

Get introduced by a VIP associated with your issue, a staff member, or just let it fly yourself. You can read from a script or notes, but try to convey as much information as you can without reading from something. You're not the president and won't be using a teleprompter, so we won't even go there. Use visuals—a chart showing the statistics, an incriminating letter, the lawsuit—and read directly from them for effect. Provide copies. Introduce people who bolster your case, but make sure you go over what they're going to say ahead of time so they don't get a case of Foot-in-Mouth and embarrass you. Stay on point and don't pontificate on unrelated issues.

Notify the press through a **Media Advisory*** and prepare a Press Release to hand out (make sure everybody gets one). Have your Spokesperson contact key reporters ahead of time and be available to them before the event, during, and after if they want to do a story. Reporters may throw some questions at you, so be prepared. For your press material, remember the classic: **Who, What, When, Where, Why, and How.**

Multi-Media: Have your presentation photographed and videoed and also do a quick clip at the end to summarize your issue. Have your supporters in the shot and record some corroborating statements from them as well. Edit the material and send it with the press release to all of the media outlets that didn't attend. Email it to your base; post to your website, Facebook and YouTube—now you're getting some traction!

Real Life Scenario: Secretary of State John Kerry took the classic to a new level when he said this about the Middle East peace process: "I'm not going to get into the who, why, what, when, where, how of why we're where we are today." Try getting all that into a press release.

Real Life Advice: Most political pros will never mention their opponents by name. If you need to reference your adversary, refer to them as "my opponent" or "the other side."

Bonus: Letting the world know you are taking the plunge to run for office is a milestone event and you'll want to make the biggest splash possible. Here are a few tips for an effective Announcement Press Conference:

Choose a location with a personal connection such as your high school or the neighborhood where you grew up. Again, it will be theatrical production, so make sure you have plenty of supporters, including family, babies, senior citizens, childhood friends, neighbors, club members, VIPs, etc. If you're running in a large district, barnstorm the countryside with multiple events.

Have a prominent figure introduce you and make sure you thank everyone for being there, including any special guests and VIPs. Don't forget your significant other, without whose support you could not succeed. Bring in a marching band or pipe in the theme from Rocky through the sound system. Generate some excitement!

Deliver your speech on why you're running and why people should vote for you. Tell the voters what you're going to do for them. Identify the key issues and how you're going to deal with them. Introduce a new initiative or two that will strike a chord with the taxpayers. Take a few potshots at your opponents if you will, but don't overdo it. Keep it brief. Hand out your palm card or brochure and a press release.

Video the event and shoot your Elevator Speech at the end while your supporters are still buzzing around. Get them in the shot and record testimonials from them as well. Take plenty of pictures. Edit the footage and get it out there.

Real Life Scenario: When business executive Meg Whitman was running for governor of California, her opponents seized on the fact that she was very wealthy (not intelligent, hard working or successful—just filthy rich). So they took to calling her "Queen Meg" and everywhere she went they sent someone dressed up like a queen to heckle her. The image was very powerful and Whitman got creamed at the polls.

 # 9 Direct Mail: A tried and true way to reach voters is through the good old U.S. Mail. What you send can come in many forms. Here's a workable series of mail messages:

• Introductory piece about you, your values, why you are running.
• More about you and some of the key issues in the race.
• Why your opponents just don't get it.
• Your vision, position on the issues.
• More on you and what you stand for; endorsements.
• Countering the negatives coming from your opponents.
• Get Out The Vote—Why it's important to vote for you.

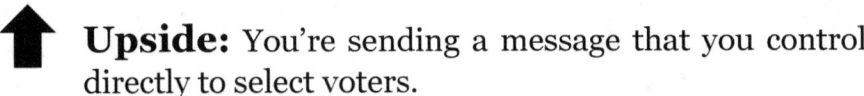

Upside: You're sending a message that you control directly to select voters.

Downside: It cost money to design, print, address and mail; it's an exercise in logistics.

**Beware:
Seconds Count**

You have only seconds to make an impression before your mail goes in the garbage, so make sure it has impact.

There are two **basic types** of campaign mail: A letter that you have to open or a flat like a postcard or larger that can be read at a glance. Your budget will limit how large your pieces will be, but no matter the size, a nice looking glossy with a powerful message will catch a voter's attention. As for letters, you'll be competing with a lot of junk mail, so give some thought to whether your presentation will induce someone to open the envelope.

Real Life Advice: It pays to use a bulk rate permit from the post office for a break on postage. Check with them first about sizes, costs and logistics. For larger efforts, a mail house* can cover everything from labeling to getting the job to the post office. For smaller productions, folding, stuffing and labeling are excellent tasks for volunteers.

As your first mailing seeks to introduce you to the voters, your opponent's opening salvo may be a negative attack on you. If it goes unchallenged and resonates with the voters, you're done. This is why some mailings have a positive, W*hy people should vote for you,* message on the front, and a negative, W*hy they shouldn't vote for the other guy,* on the reverse. If you go negative first, your opponent will probably devote his next few pieces to come back at you.

For the newcomer, you will want to educate the voters on who you are and what you bring to the table before you start cutting down the other side. Let your campaign budget guide you. If you can afford five mailings, use the first two to establish yourself and half of the next one to criticize your opponent and the other half to offer yourself as a better alternative. Depending how the race is going, you can make the fourth piece entirely negative and devote the final mailing to yourself. If there are distinct differences between you and your opponent, highlight them—just be prepared for a counter attack. Go to **www.WinAnElection.org** for some great examples.

Negative Campaigning: This is as good a time as any to talk about going after your opponent and how to handle incoming attacks. American politics has a rich history of candidates making personal, destructive remarks about each other and it really hasn't stopped since our founding fathers first started in. After all, it was our third president, Thomas Jefferson, who thought he could score some points against John Adams by accusing him of having a...

...hideous hermaphroditical character, which has neither the force and firmness of a man, nor the gentleness and sensibility of a woman.

Before you start slinging mud, think about how the public—and your opponent—will react. If you reference something ridiculous like a person's hideous hermaphroditical character, the voters will shrug it off and think you're a loon. Plus, such rhetoric comes off as desperate and will undermine your creditability.

But what about something more germane like your opponent's record? Generally speaking, personal attacks usually backfire while commentary on someone's public performance will plant a seed in the voter's mind. In fact, if you're new to the scene, the other side will try to define you in a way that vastly differs from your version.

If you're going to attack, make your case clearly and back it up with facts:

> *Councilman Amato voted to raise taxes 17 times**
> *last year making it harder and harder for our*
> *seniors and young people to live here.*
>
> *Source: Town Council voting records

Of course, Councilman Amato is going to counter:

> *The fact is, I have a long record of cutting taxes.*
> *My opponent, who has no record at all in govern-*
> *ment, should get her facts straight and maybe at-*
> *tend a town board meeting once in a while to find*
> *out what's really going on.*

Real Life Scenario: In his book, Courage and Consequence, Karl Rove details how he helped get George W.
Bush elected governor of Texas and then president. He
talks about focusing negative campaigning not on a person's weaknesses, but on what they think are their
strengths. Al Gore, he notes, thought he had a superior in-
tellect, so he was portrayed as someone who looks down on
the average voter. John Kerry thought he was strong on defense until the Swift Boat Veterans for Truth highlighted his
anti-war comments. The attacks were made even more
powerful by using the target's own words against them.

In the final analysis, your ability to attack and counterattack boils down to the resources you have available to reach the voters. If your opponent has the funds to send nine negative mail pieces and you can only afford two, you'll be at a distinct disadvantage. If your area enjoys a robust local press and they're covering the race blow by blow, then your point-counterpoint will get plenty of air time. At the end of the day, however, voters will tune out the negative and want to know what you're bringing to the table, so make sure you have ways to tell your positive story.

Real Life Advice: Create a Rapid Response Team to quickly act when your opponent or his minions slam you. Don't sit idly by as they dominate the conversation. Adjust your mailing and advertising; call a press conference or put out a white paper stating the facts. There are numerous chat rooms, rumor boards, and other venues where people can post opinions and refute your opponent. At the first hint of trouble, ask key supporters to post commentary favorable to you (and negative to your opponent). Have them respond to press coverage and post on Facebook, tweet, etc. to keep the discussion going in your favor.

Beware: Consider the Source

If you uncover some salacious detail about your opponent's sordid past, be careful how you use it. People will usually consider the source, so maybe it would be best for the skeleton to be let out of the closet by somebody else.

Real Life Scenario: President Nixon resigned in disgrace following Watergate, a scandal involving a break in at the Democrat headquarters. Ironically, Nixon's campaign didn't need to resort to spying. He won reelection by a landslide anyway. The moral of the story is that dirty tricks usually end in disaster and probably won't help the cause.

#10 Advertising: Radio ads, TV commercials and newspaper spreads are an excellent way to build name recognition and get your message out, but you have to pay for them. Analyze your budget to see what you can afford. Take a look at the options. If, for example, your area has a radio station everyone listens to, it would be a good bet to get on there. But what if your region is covered by a few different stations? Should you go on the easy listening station, all news, classic rock? Again, the money's going to add up fast and maybe it would be better spent on direct mail.

Upside: Advertising can spread your message far and wide.
Downside: You have to pay for it.

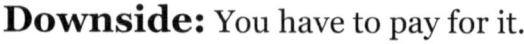

Is your area dominated by a single daily newspaper or are there a few weeklies? Do the major television stations originate from a large city and your district is on the far end of their broadcast area? If so, you're going to pay a lot of money to advertise to a lot of people who can't vote for you. An advertising agency should be able to sort it all out, create a budget and help design your ads. You can also gather the facts by contacting each media outlet yourself. Either way, you'll need to figure out the biggest bang for your buck.

Name Recognition: Everybody knows who Bill Clinton is, but who the heck is Mary Morgan? Billions are spent on brand recognition for Coca Cola, Budweiser, and Chevrolet and political candidates are no different, except you don't have billions.

Signs and posters with your picture on them are a cheap and effective way of matching the name with the face. It's the same with your palm card and electronic images (they don't call it Facebook for nothing). Here's a quick list of items you can order to get your name out there (Google "campaign supplies" and have your credit card ready):

Bags, balloons, bookmarks, bumper stickers, buttons, clips, combs, doorknob hangers, golf tees, jar openers, key chains, letter openers, magnets, nail files, pads, pencils, pens, posters, pot holders, rulers, stickers, yard signs, etc.

Real Life Scenario: A candidate marched in a popular Fourth of July parade and after a few steps, realized nobody had a clue who he was. Thousands of people saw him waiving and smiling, but it didn't help his name recognition. The next time he was in a parade, he had two young nieces walk in front of him holding a banner: Jim Mazur, Candidate for the County Legislature.

 # 11 The Internet and Social Media brings us to the fastest growing and most impactful campaign techniques since Lyndon Johnson went on TV with the "Daisy Girl" ad in 1964 (Check it out on YouTube—it'll blow your mind). The tech world has given the office seeker some serious tools so, if you haven't yet, drag your knuckles into the 21st Century and get on board.

 Upside: Affordable and effective.
Downside: High maintenance.

Real Life Scenario: The majority of voters under 50 now receive their news online, according to the Pew Research Center for People and the Press, and the younger they are, the more they rely on the web for information—not newspapers, TV, or radio. The Internet, particularly Social Media, has changed the world and the candidates who tap it for all its worth will have a distinct advantage.

Technology in political races is important, but it's not rocket science. Have no fear and just follow these tips and you will be posting like a pro!

Let's take it from the top:

Website: The Internet is the first place savvy voters will go to find out about the election and candidates and if you don't have a website, or yours looks like crap, you are instantly at a disadvantage. There are many companies and Internet providers that can walk you through the steps to create a credible web presence. Remember, credibility is the key. It's the same as if you dress shabbily or deliver unrehearsed speeches—Your website must make you look like a serious contender. If it doesn't, you're a has-been.

Facebook: It's not a multi-billion dollar phenomenon for nothing. People interact on Facebook hundreds of millions of times a day. Your campaign must have a Facebook presence and you should consistently post salient, interesting messages to build your fan base. Your website should have a link to your Facebook page where you can give the voters a clear understanding of who you are and what you're going to do for them. Again, credibility is key so have a nice "banner" at the top with your A-game photo and some nice graphics. Any teen can set it up. Facebook also has an advertising platform. Contact them to see what they can do for you.

Real Life Advice: In this age of electronic media, your graphic image says a lot about you. Websites, Social Media, emails, even your stationary and press releases require a header with your campaign logo, slogan, photo, and a nice font. Have a designer work something out and make sure it's sharp, appropriate, and professional. This is the first thing people will notice when you communicate with them and will be featured on most everything you do. If it doesn't scream credibility, as campaign guru Ron Nehring says, people won't be impressed.

Twitter: Believe it or not, as your campaign progresses, there will be people interested in your daily activities. In addition to posting on Facebook, you can tweet messages to your followers on Twitter. If you get "retweeted" to a follower's list—and maybe even retweeted again—the amount of people hearing your pearls of wisdom can grow exponentially. A photo-sharing site that's quite popular is Instagram—check it out. Like anything else on the Internet, keep your posts salient and interesting or people will tune out.

YouTube: Once you have your stump speech on par with President Obama's, have someone video it. From there it's quit a simple matter to upload the footage to YouTube and provide links from your website, emails, etc. Wheel off a passionate defense of your position on the mega mall and get it out there. Post testimonial clips of your supporters explaining why they're voting for you. YouTube allows you to add key words to your video postings, so if someone searches "mega mall," your piece will come up—what an effective way to get your message to the masses!

Show Me the Money: If a light bulb hasn't yet popped in your head, please note that these techniques are extraordinary door openers for fundraising. People you cultivate a relationship with through Social Media will donate if you ask, so make sure your website has a place where they can safely give to the cause. For instance, those involved in the mega mall battle will stay tuned if you keep them informed and will pony up because you are fighting their fight.

Email Lists—The Holy Grail: To really judge an organization's commitment to you, see if they'll give you a copy of their email data base. Most times they won't because a) They don't want to hand over such a valuable resource or b) Their list is so paltry they're embarrassed to let anyone see it. If the name of the game is contacting potential supporters for money, peoplepower, and votes, a group's email list is a great place to start. If they won't give you the data, feed them a steady stream of emails they can forward to their membership and make sure you include links back to your website so you can sign up these contacts to your own list.

Email is an easy and effective way to stay in touch with your supporters. Companies such as Constant Contact, Elite Mail, and Mail Chimp have broken this down to a science and offer ready-made templates that will professionalize your messages. They will help you maintain your contact lists and provide support for most anything you want to do such as raise money and GOTV. Keep the mice clicking by linking people to your website and Social Media right from your email.

Google: Another multi-billion-dollar enterprise is Google which enables people to find just about anything online. What appears when you Google yourself? What about your election or the issues at hand? Will your material pop up or will the advantage go to your opponent? The way it works is the more information you put out into cyberspace—through your website, Facebook, Twitter, blogs, videos, articles, etc.—the higher you will rank in the search engines and the more people you will be exposed to. The word "expose" is most appropriate since everything about you, good or bad, will show up and the only way to drive away the bad stuff on the Internet is to constantly populate the good.

Remember, in developing your on-line persona, **Creativity is King**. Keep your media alive with new, imaginative, pertinent, real information and people will stay engaged. And when it comes time to ask them to promote you to their peeps or give you money, you will have crafted relationships worth their weight in gold.

> **Bonus:** Go to Google Alerts (if you can't find it, Google it) and set up searches for your name and the campaign—might as well throw your opponent in there as well. Each time something pertaining to these "key words" appears on the Internet such as a news article or a post, you will receive an alert via email.

Campaigning Goes High Tech: Remember those people going door to door? How about now they're holding iPods or Smart phones with a map of the neighborhood and the home they need to go to next right on the screen? If the voter says they're with you, the walker enters that vital little factoid into the app and the system transmits it to a data base to make sure they're on your GOTV list. If they're with the other guy, the system removes them and if they're undecided, they go into another category altogether.

Campaigning Goes Back to Basics: Since every voter counts, why not enroll a few of your own? If you have 10 people working on your race and you challenge them to register 10 new voters each, that's 100 people who will probably cast a ballot for you. Add them to your database with a "new voter" tag and send them a letter congratulating them for taking the first step toward participating in our democracy. Follow that up with a GOTV letter.

Bonus I: If you're running under a particular party, enroll the new voters under that party. This way, you'll swell the ranks of the organization and the enrollees will be able to vote for you in a primary.

Bonus II: There's no question that immigrants continue to flood into the United States and have an impact on electoral politics. Run from these groups at your own peril, especially if your opponent is enrolling them. Would a minority voter plank with an aggressive voter registration component fit into your plans?

If the person who signed up some new voters makes sure they get to the polls, your **Voter Registration Drive** will have created some votes out of thin air. Keep in mind most elections have deadline for new registrants. If the enrollment forms have to be in by a certain day, make sure you don't blow it.

Another low-tech effort that pays dividends is an **Absentee Voter Program.** Most elections make provisions for people who can't get to the polls and want to vote by absentee ballot. Normally, they have to request the ballot ahead of time and send it back by a certain date. This system generates a voter list, so get your hands on it and send them two letters: One, congratulating them for taking the steps necessary to participate in our democracy and Two, right when the ballots go out, another congratulating them again and urging them to vote for you.

Many absentee voters serve in the military and are stationed far from home, so give your letters a patriotic flair. Better yet, have them come from a veteran writing on your behalf. Indeed, it is the sacrifice of these selfless warriors that protects our precious right to vote.

Some seniors are homebound or in nursing homes and can't get out to vote. As callous as it seems, campaigns target these areas for absentee votes and in a close race, you'd be damned glad to have them.

Finally, everyone associated with your campaign needs to fill out **Do Me a Favor Cards.** These are pre-printed post cards your supporters can send to people they know urging them to vote. Have them go over the voter lists and flag every friend and acquaintance. Address the cards by hand and write a personal note. A few dozen people doing hundreds of these really adds up. Of course, when Election Day rolls around, they have to make sure their people vote. Look at the sample in the Appendix.

Real Life Scenario: One councilman handed out pads printed with his name and face on them with the slogan: "Gene Gerrard, He's on Our Side." Voters were reminded of him, sheet after sheet.

The team settled in for a strategy meeting to go over which of the 11 tactics they would focus on to get Mary's message to the voters.

The candidate dedicated herself to knocking on doors and looked forward to dropping a few pounds by putting in some mileage. Rob and Bernard broke up the district into manageable chunks and Max went to work with Betty to schedule volunteers to accompany her. (See Chapter Eleven to find out how they built their contact lists). Mary had her Elevator Speech down pat and people were receptive. She was armed with a palm card to hand to voters—including a special one for the mega mall area—and a doorknob hanger to leave in case people weren't home.

Mary's walking lists had space where she could notate if the voter was with her or not. The campaign updated the data base to indicate those expected to go Mary's way and flagged the ones who flat out said they were opposed. These would be ignored in the GOTV drive.

The campaign also generated phone lists for the volunteers to hammer away on and for Mary to call when she wasn't walking. They featured a voter ID component to support the GOTV program. Max had secured 10 different locations with a total of 60 phones to keep the lines buzzing.

"They love it when I stop by the phone banks to thank the volunteers," Mary told the team. "I make sure they have enough to eat and drink."

"We have a secret weapon for the three days before the election," Rob reported. "Congressman Poplar has agreed to record a get-out-the-vote robo call message. Every one of our targeted voters is going to hear from him."

"Splendid," Carol replied. "He gets elected by huge numbers every time. I'm sure some of his popularity will rub off on Mary."

"We have the message up on Mary's site along with a picture of her and the congressman," Bernard added. "It's getting some nice hits."

Next up was Betty with a printout of Mary's schedule from Google Docs. "We have 17 events for Mary to attend between now and Election Day. Has everyone been able to get into the schedule on line?"

"Yes, it's perfect," Max said. "I'll use it to make sure Mary has an entourage everywhere she goes."

"It also makes my job a cinch," said Pete, Mary's Driver. "I can check it on my iPhone and get Mary where she's got to go. I may add: Betty, thanks for putting the contact information in there. Yesterday we were running a little late for the Friends of the Library meeting and I called them and they said, 'no problem.'"

"That meeting went well," Mary added. "We were able to recruit three new volunteers and they were nice enough to give us their membership list, on a CD no less."

"Already entered it into the data base and a thank you letter is on its way," Betty reported.

Rob went over Mary's direct mail campaign, noting that the budget will allow for seven pieces. Four would highlight Mary while two would rough up her opponent. The final mailing would urge people to get out and vote. Rob was happy to announce that the budget would allow for large, glossy post-card style pieces.

"Check it out," he said, unveiling a 9"x12" prototype.

"Impressive!"

"Anything else on the advertising front?" Carol asked.

"Yes, we have a pretty decent radio buy on WCVW and they've agreed to have Mary on for three live interviews, the last being Saturday before the election. We also have ads on Facebook and bought some Google AdWords to direct people interested in the race to our site."

"Sweet."

"We also reserved four billboards on the two main roads into town."

"Those are huge," Lou commented. "Larger than life!"

"We've also got seven ads in the Centerville Post— they've been pretty good to us so far and we want to keep it that way," Rob said. "Maybe we can get an endorsement out of them."

Bernard said the Internet and Social Media platforms were banging on all cylinders.

"The hits on Mary's website are showing that people are going there for election information and our likes on Facebook are growing every day," he said. "Plus, people are getting a kick out of Mary's daily tweets and YouTube videos. Judging from their comments, it sounds like they really feel like they're part of the campaign."

Bernard added, "By the way, money is rolling in through our online donation platform and we have a pretty healthy email data base going."

Carol smiled and so did Mary.

"I did a Google search on the council race and Mary dominates," Lou piped up. "Nice work, Bernard."

Max chimed back in: "I want to throw out some kudos to my nephew, Michael, for heading up the voter registration drive and our absentee ballot effort. He's registered 100 new voters so far and one of his friends, a veteran, will do a letter to the absentee voters in the military. Every vote counts and we're leaving no stone unturned."

"Well done!"

"Wait, there's more," Max continued. "Mike's also picking up a lot of new minority voters, people who seem quite pleased they get to vote. I'm pretty sure they will go our way."

Finally, Linda reported that Mary's announcement press conference in front of town hall was a big hit. About 50 supporters showed up thanks to Max making a bunch of phone calls, and the campaign got a ton of photos with people holding Mary Morgan signs in front of a great backdrop. The campaign colors made the event look patriotic.

Rob had the event videotaped and they did a few takes of the candidate explaining why people should vote for her. Bernard had the footage on YouTube right away and Carol used it in an email fundraising pitch.

A reporter from the Centerville Post showed up to the announcement press conference, probably because Linda and Mary dropped in on the editor beforehand, as well as a radio reporter and a crew from the local cable news station. Bernard posted links from Mary's website to the news coverage.

"They used most of our stuff verbatim," Linda said tapping Mary's press kit.

The candidate tweeted: "Great story about campaign in Centerville Post. Please retweet." She used www.Bitly.com to shorten the URL for the story and Bernard showed her how to paste it into the tweet. Later, Bernard went to Bitly to find out how many people clicked through to the article. There were a lot.

"The race is on!" Linda exclaimed, pumping her fist in the air. The rest of the team did the same.

CHAPTER TEN
SPECIAL CAMPAIGN UPDATE
THE PRIMARY ELECTION

Carol tracked down Kingsley and practically had to beat out of him who the Democrats were going to support. It was Fink. He pressed Carol to see if Mary was considering a primary election.

"That's for us to know and you to find out," she told him as she slammed down the phone.

The Centerville Post was on the other line.

"They want to know if Mary's running a primary," Betty called out to the team.

"Well Mary, what do you think?" Rob asked, his hand over the mouthpiece. "If you don't run, the campaign is over and we'll all have to pack up and go home."

Mary grabbed the phone: "I'm in all the way."

The next step was drafting nominating petitions and Mary and Carol went to see Henry Bratton again. Somehow, he knew they were coming and had a petition sheet already prepared.

"Print as many copies as you need and make sure you get them signed only by Democrats," he advised them. "You need two hundred signatures, but try to get three hundred or more in case some of them are bad. Whoever signs, they have to use their full name, no initials or nicknames."

"Got it," Mary said. "Thank you."

Bratton added, "Make sure the date is filled in when the person signed and don't forget to get the petitions to the board of elections by June second."

For $25, the campaign received a CD of voter data from the board of elections and Rob and Bernard crunched it to produce lists of Democrats broken down by street. They printed up cards with directions for each volunteer. Max Baumgartner organized the petition drive and in no time they collected over 300 signatures. He gave Mary a progress report.

"It sounds like we have enough," Mary said. "Let's submit them a day early to show we mean business."

Proudly, Mary, Rob and Max went to the BOE that afternoon to submit the petitions.

"Just fill out this form and clip the petitions together," the clerk told them. "You got them in without a minute to spare."

"What do you mean," Mary replied. "Isn't tomorrow the deadline?"

"Oh no. It's today, June 1. Mr. Fink had his in yesterday."

"What about Madeline Shott?"

"We haven't heard anything from her."

"I think Bratton purposely gave us the wrong date," Mary said in the parking lot.

A few days later, the campaign received a registered letter from the board of elections. Betty signed for it.

"Your petitions for Centerville Town Council District 3 have been disqualified due to the following reason(s):

"Insufficient office description...failure to specify Council District number."

Rob shot over to the BOE and was told Mary's petition referenced the town council, but did not specify that she was running in the 3rd district. A complaint had been filed by Mr. Fink and, acting on that complaint, the election commissioners invalidated her petitions.

That night, the campaign team met to discuss the day's events.

"It was that bastard Bratton," Carol declared. "I knew there was something about him I didn't like."

"Not only did he give us a bad petition, but he gave us the wrong date," Mary added. "If we didn't go today we would have missed the deadline."

They decided to hire a lawyer to try and get Mary on the primary ballot and disqualify Fink's petitions. Rob was familiar with election law attorney Marvin Adler and knew him to be a straight shooter, so they brought him on board.

The next day brought another surprise. Fink sent out a mailing attacking Mary for being weak on economic development and creating jobs. The two-sided flat didn't mention the mega mall by name, but stated:

"Morgan stands in the way of beneficial economic projects and job creation for our young people and working families."

It threw in another dig: "If she can't even get her paperwork straight to run for office how can she possibly be on the town council?"

Mary was livid. She wasn't even on the ballot and Fink was taking shots at her.

"Welcome to the wonderful world of politics," Rob told her.

Since the election wouldn't wait, Mary's lawyer had to work fast. He filed a motion in county court seeking to validate Mary's petitions and get her on the ballot. He also scrutinized Fink's paperwork. Sure enough, he had language specifying the third district—the critical fact Bratton left out of Mary's petition. Fink had 265 more names than he needed and, Adler concluded, it would be next to impossible to knock him off the ballot.

"How much is all this legal action going to cost?" Mary wanted to know.

"I had a feeling we were going to need some legal help so we planned for it in the budget," Rob replied. "If our fundraising stays on track, and you don't get tired of dialing for dollars, we can get through the primary with a little left over for the general election."

"The hell with the general election," Mary said, banging her hand on the desk. "I don't want to leave anything on the table. Let's go after Fink with everything we got and then we can raise more money after I win. It should be a little easier if I'm the official candidate."

"As you wish, Madam Councilwoman," Rob said with a smile. He had Linda send out a press release castigating Fink for his underhanded moves and followed it up with a mailing to all of Centerville's Democrats.

"Don Fink and the political bosses don't want to give you a choice in the Democratic primary for the Centerville council," the piece read. "Are they afraid to leave this important decision up to you? Say no to backroom deals. Tell Don Fink to let the voters decide."

Adler reported in: "The country court judge, a Democrat, let the board of elections decision stand."

Mary was still off the ballot.

"Nothing but a political hack judge," Adler said, recommending that Mary file an appeal.

"Strike two," Adler phoned into campaign headquarters a week later. A three-judge appellate panel ruled 2-1 against overturning the first ruling. "The decision's actually good news," the attorney said.

"We lost," Mary replied. "How is this good news?"

"The third justice was on our side and remarked that in cases like these, the decision should be left to the voters. This opens the door to an appeal with the state's highest court."

"How much is this going to run us?"

"Don't worry," Rob said. "We've got it covered."

Fink's lawyer fought Adler tooth and nail and he also had to contend with a "friend of the court" attorney sent over by the Democrats.

"What a schmuck," Adler said of the Democrat lawyer. "They certainly wasted their money on him."

It was less than six weeks before Primary Day and Adler asked the appellate judges to expedite their decision. It was unanimous. The people who signed Mary's petition were aware they were signing to have her run for the town council, the judges noted.

"In this case," they ruled, "it would be best to let the voters decide."

"We won!" Marvin texted Mary from the state capitol. "Congratulations and good luck with your election."

Bernard reported that night at the campaign meeting:

"The court battle stirred up quite an interest in the race. Our website hits have quadrupled and we're lighting it up on Facebook and Twitter. Money's coming in and we're picking up followers and volunteers left and right. They made a big mistake trying to keep us off the ballot."

"Yeah, they thought it was business as usual," Rob replied. "They didn't think we could capitalize on it like we did."

"There's something happening that's pretty interesting," Bernard added. "We're getting more seniors on Facebook than I thought we would. Do you know why?"

"I do," Rob replied. "They're on there because Facebook's the only way they can keep up with their grandchildren who have moved away because their families can't afford to live here."

"Exactly."

"Make sure we speak to them directly," Rob said.

"You bet."

Next item of business: the tracking poll results. Rob asked the pollster to survey Democrats in Mary's district who voted in Centerville's last two primaries. "Mary's neck and neck with Fink overall, but she's doing better than him with women voters," Rob read from the poll. "Seniors are leaning toward Mary, though Fink has the edge with younger voters who can't find work."

The poll revealed that environmental issues are strong, but there is an overall sense of worry about the economy and jobs. Seniors bemoaned the high cost of living and taxes. The poll also found that among women, there was worry about education issues and parks and recreation services for their kids. Opposition to the mega mall in a 10-block radius around the site was off the charts. For the rest of the district, it was 55-45 against.

Based on the tracking poll, Rob created a mailing to all Democrats on Mary's economic and jobs creation plan. It mentioned the area's substandard job statistics and took a shot at Fink for his work at the development agency. He also targeted pieces to:

- Senior citizens on Mary's plan to rein in government spending and cut taxes.
- Women on the importance of families and education, including her plan to revitalize the town's park facilities.
- Voters near the mega mall site reiterating Mary's opposition.

The president of the Centerville League of Conservation Voters sent out a letter on Mary's behalf, as did the economics professor, Dr. Morton Blackstein. Fink had construction unions and some state politicians go to bat for him and wasn't shy about pointing out that he, not Mary, was the choice of the Centerville Dem-ocratic Party.

Mary countered with a mailer urging people to "Say no to the hand-selected candidate of the political bosses." It also mentioned that Fink's been a member of the Industrial Development Agency for 10 years and his record on attracting new business and creat-ing jobs has been pretty lousy.

Rob reminded the team that a primary is a Get Out The Vote exercise and the race will be won by Mary's troops. They called a meeting with Max.

"You're in good shape," Max told Mary. "You have about a dozen solid volunteers from the Rotary Club and another 50 from friends of friends. We've got 10 phone bank locations and they're making calls every night. Tomorrow we start going door-to-door. Where are you going to be?"

"We've got Mary scheduled to go out almost every night," Rob answered. "I hope you don't mind if we wear you out," he said looking at the candidate.

"I'm game. As long as there are people with me and we can make an impact, I'll knock on as many doors as I can."

"I've been monitoring your schedule in Google Docs," Max said. "Rest assured, our people will be there wherever you go."
"I heard Fink hates going door-to-door," Lou reported.

"Great," said Mary. "Let's go out there and kick his butt."

"One last thing," the Campaign Manager said, "and I hope I'm not asking too much. Here's a list of some donors. We need you to call them and get more money."

"Okay. It's not my favorite thing to do, but people have been receptive so I'll keep at it." Mary was pleased to know that Carol and a few others would be making calls along with her.

Mary's signs sprang up like mushrooms on the lawns of her supporters and she made the rounds of the civic groups, Democrat clubs, and environmental organizations. Mary and her opponent crossed paths at a few events and were cordial to each other, though Mary thought she had better handouts—nail files, combs, and little pads with her name on them. There were no debates.

The primary election didn't exactly light the media world on fire and the coverage was minimal. Linda couldn't get the Centerville Post to make an endorsement, though they did run some letters to the editor and a synopsis of the race to remind people to vote.

Bernard reported that Fink's campaign failed to grasp the power of the Internet and had a "lame" online presence. Mary, on the other hand, was going full tilt and picked up volunteers and online donations through her website and Facebook page. She kept her followers updated through Twitter and some of her tweets were retweeted, picking her up even more fol-lowers. Her email donation appeals raised enough money to fund two more mailings and she went after the younger voters and women again with messages tailored to their issues.

The polls opened at nine in the morning and would run until nine at night. Mary's door knocking and phone operation identified 500 voters who said they are leaning her way and her troops focused on them the first thing in the morning. They were offered rides to the polls and at six o'clock, Mary's poll watchers made a list of those who hadn't yet voted. Volunteers were dispatched to their homes. Mary, Carol, Max, Rob and everyone else associated with the campaign burned up the phones.

"Today's an important day for Centerville," they told the voters, "and we hope you will do your part. Please vote for Mary Morgan in the Democrat primary. She's the only one with a solid economic plan and job crea-tion strategy and she cares about our senior citizens, working families and young people. Can we count on your vote for Mary today?"

The campaign had also sent letters thanking Mary's petition signers and they made a concerted effort to get those voters to the polls as well.

Bernard had amassed an email list of 1,147 people and he sent out a total of seven messages leading up to the primary. On the day of the vote, he did three more encouraging people to exercise their constitu-tional right (and remind their family, friends, and neighbors to vote as well). The video and photos from Mary's announcement press conference added to her credibility.

Through it all, Mary's husband, Tom, was a trooper, offering Mary emotional support and showing up at the headquarters from time to time to say hello and contact the Democrats he knew from the voter lists.

Linda staged a photo with Mary casting her ballot and talked a photographer from The Centerville Post into coming down. Bernard got the photo out over every platform.

Centerville has electronic voting machines where people mark their choices on a computer card which is scanned by an optical reader. The poll results came in quickly. By 9:30, the count was reported: Mary trounced Fink with 60 percent of the vote! A few minutes later, he made a concession call wishing her well. People they had never seen before began showing up at the campaign headquarters. A significant no show, however, was Kingsley, the Democrat leader.

The campaign headquarters was jubilant—Mary's first win! Linda shot a quick video of Mary thanking her supporters and saying she looked forward to running on her platform of improving Centerville's economy, creating jobs, and making sure the town's seniors and young people are taken care of. Linda sent out a press release and Bernard blasted Mary's message far and wide.

Rob sent everyone home by eleven. "We start all over again tomorrow, but this time it will be with our new friend, Big Mo."*

CHAPTER ELEVEN
BUILDING A
WINNING MAJORITY

11

To win your election, you'll need to employ some basic math. Theoretically, one vote is all it takes, but you don't want to cut it that close, and your goal should be getting as many votes as you can. In campaign parlance, 51 percent of the vote beats 49 percent, though you would rather make it 60-40 or even 65-35 since your margin of victory, or plurality,* will have great bearing on your strength as an office holder.

In fact, elected officials like to claim a "mandate"* for the issues they ran on and use it to push through their agendas. Plus, the public will have more confidence in—and your colleagues and foes will have more respect for—a person who wins big, rather than just squeaks by. And a close race gives your opponents motivation to go after you the next time around.

In order to hit the magic number, the pros identify **blocs**—groups of voters they'll need to win—and build contact lists so the campaign can go after them. From here, it becomes a mathematical exercise: If certain percentages of one group or another go your way, you win. Political consultants make a science out of narrowing down the groups and focusing their efforts on winning percentages. They analyze past voter performance, precinct turnout, and other factors to create a roadmap for success. You don't have to get that crazy—a little knowledge about where to plumb for your votes, however, will go a long way.

Real Life Scenario: In the 2012 presidential race, the two sides boiled down the Swing Voters down to just a handful of states. Swing state Nevada, for example, was deluged with mailings, advertisements, and candidate visits, while New York, a safe Blue State for the Democrats, was ignored.

Swing Voters can come from any party, but many times are independents or blanks* who take their right to vote seriously. They spend more time thinking about the election than most and put some effort into figuring out who's the better candidate. On Election Day, they give statisticians fits by voting for a Democrat in one race, a Republican in another, and none of the above in others.

Opposite of the Swing Voter is what talk show host Rush Limbaugh calls the **"Low Information"** voter, someone who has bought into a certain candidate or philosophy lock, stock, and barrel and will never change their mind no matter what.

Real Life Scenario: In one of the most incredible vote tallies of all time, Al Gore actually outpolled George Bush for the White House. But because the Electoral College gives weighted votes to each state, Bush was able to take the presidency by winning the states. The whole race came down to Florida where the two were in a virtual dead heat. It took the U.S. Supreme Court to break the deadlock and serves as an historic example of why every vote counts.

Is your race partisan? In other words, are the candidates coming from established political parties such as Republican or Democrat, or are they running under unique labels such as the Centerville First Team?

In a partisan election, you can expect a certain level of support from the voters in your party. However, don't expect to win just because your area always elects Democrats and you're a Democrat. Just like in a non-partisan race, many will vote for

> **Real Life Scenario:** California has been a Democratic Blue State* since the 1930's, yet five of the last 8 governors have been Republican. In those exact same elections, guess how many Republican lieutenant governors were voted in? None. This shows that high visibility races move people to carefully consider the candidates before making their decision. For the less visible lieutenant governor, voters didn't care and defaulted to their party. For the head of the ticket, a crucial portion of Democrats decided to cross party lines and vote Republican. These Swing Voters* and ticker splitters* must be taken into consideration in building your winning coalition.

the person. They will sum you up, consider your narrative, see what you are about and what you have to offer, especially if your race is high visibility and people are paying attention.

In non-partisan elections, voters will focus even more on you as the candidate since you won't be running under the label of an established party. Voters will zero in on your background and more closely scrutinize your platform. Building your majority with groups where you share a common thread will give you a great advantage.

This is why you should spend so much time developing your persona and your message and the techniques you'll need to connect with the voters. Assuming people will vote for you just because you're a member of their party is risky business.

Getting the Data: The authority that administers elections in your area such as the board of elections or village clerk should have a list of enrolled voters, as well as past election results and a record of who actually voted. Make a formal request and see if you can get the information on a disk in a spreadsheet format. This will make it easier to break down the data. You can get up to speed pretty easily on spreadsheet programs such as Excel or Access and this knowledge will take you far.

Beware: Don't Be FOILed

Some jurisdictions may require you to file a Freedom of Information Law (FOIL)* request for voter data. So make sure you start the process as early as possible in case they stall.

Real Life Scenario: There are companies that maintain voter data, including phone numbers, which the official sources may not provide. Many of these firms are politically oriented and can provide valuable campaign advice along with the lists. When it comes right down to it, however, you may have to run down phone numbers and email addresses yourself—that's what volunteers are for.

For your other targeted groups, membership lists with names, addresses, emails and phone numbers are worth their weight in gold. Events such as the anti-mega mall rally are ideal places to collect contact information. Circulate sign-up sheets and make sure everyone signs in.

Piece by Piece: To build your winning list of voters, start with your platform. If you're in it to fight the mega mall, that's the first piece of the puzzle. Environmental groups related to the fight will also support you. If you're tough on crime, people in high crime areas will see things your way and if you want to improve parks and playgrounds, people with young families will go for you. If you live in the suburbs, local voters will lean toward you and if you are a member of a specific organization, church, or service group, you can mine that commonality as well.

Bloc Heads: Search out the unique voting blocs in your area such as soccer moms,* religious groups, gun advocates, environmentalists—you name it—that can deliver the margin of difference for you. These groups key in on issues important to them and ignore most everything else. Do you relate?

Real Life Advice: No one with your campaign should leave the house without a stack of **"I'm With You, Mary!"** cards to collect contact information. Entered into your database, these contacts will be a valuable well of support when you need it most. The cards should also have boxes people can check off if they want to volunteer, contribute, host an event, etc. An email version of the card should be produced so people can reach out to potential supporters online. See the Appendix for an example.

For smaller races, you can really fine tune the groups you'll need to win. Everyone who showed up to complain about the luxurious new firehouse would be inclined to vote for you if you were running as a commissioner against wasteful spending, while firemen who would use the new building will go for the candidate who supports it. There may be a neighborhood of people who don't want the facility near their homes. Maybe there's an unpopular fire chief and there are people who hate him. The point is, the more you bore into what's going on, the easier it will be to design a winning plan.

You can pander to voting blocs, but only to the point where you don't offend your base, which may not agree with their issues. The knitting together of voting groups, while not overtly alienating or offending anyone else, is a critical skill for a politician.

For a partisan race, do some historical homework. Look at the vote tallies in particular election districts or precincts. Did the Republicans win one year and the Democrats the next, or has it been reliably Republican? If you're a Republican, add those reliable districts to your list. If the voters flip flop, add them as well and get them to flip your way. If they've always gone Democrat, don't waste your effort unless the rest of your plan requires that you get at least some votes from these areas.

The voting public is not the same as the population. If your area has more young people than seniors, don't assume more young people will vote. In fact, seniors go to the polls more frequently than the younger population.

You can use voter data to narrow down your targets with great accuracy. If 10,000 people routinely hit the polls across 10 districts, how can you break these districts down to get the 5,001 votes you'll need to win? Start adding it up. Identify the districts that reliably go your party's way and calculate the votes you can expect. How many votes will you now need from the swing areas? Is it doable? Add in what you'll get from the opposing districts. Now an accurate picture is starting to form. Break it down into percentages. If 65 percent of the voters in the reliable districts go your way and you win 60 percent of the Swing Voters, what percentage do you need to win in the opposing districts to hit 5,001?

Massaging the numbers to figure out where you need your votes to come from has been honed to an art form by Front Line's Ron Nehring, the former California GOP chair and lieutenant governor candidate. He breaks down the "granularity" of the electorate and can determine where you should spend your resources and what areas are lost causes. Ron can break down these subsets with stunning accuracy, so it may pay to bring in the experts to help you figure it all out.

Real Life Scenario: If your opponent is spending an inordinate amount of time in areas that have always voted your party line, then they: a) Have limitless resources and are messing with you, b) Don't know what they're doing, or c) Have a game plan that requires them to take away a certain percentage of votes from your base.

While it's tempting to contact all of your opponent's supporters to get them to see the light, its best to stay with your base and areas that have shown they could swing your way. Don't take your built-in constituencies for granted. If you are running as a Democrat, go see the Democrats identified in your analysis. Make sure they hear from you. Make sure they vote. Some candidates fail because they ignore their base and spend too much time courting people who would never vote for them anyway. Stay loyal to your voting blocs; turn out the voters naturally aligned with you.

Trying to take votes from your opponent can be tricky because the more you appeal to voters on the other side of the isle, the more you risk losing your base. Politicians walk these fine lines all the time. If you are running as a Conservative and you start appealing to the Liberals, you will lose the Conservatives. Stay in the middle on all the issues and you appeal to neither side. There is an upside to poaching votes from your opponent, however—each vote counts as two: One for you and one your opponent lost.

When analyzing the data, don't forget voter turnout. If the majority of a district is from your party, but voter turnout is usually low, a strong GOTV effort may be in order.

Last but not least: Factor in the new registrants, especially the ones your campaign signed up. Maybe they'll be your margin of victory!

CAMPAIGN UPDATE

Rob and Bernard went back to work on the voter CD from the board of elections. Centerville is broken down into four council districts and within the third, Mary's district, there are 10 precincts. The first thing they did was pull a list of all registered voters in the area where the mega mall was proposed. The data indicated which of the registrants actually voted in the last five elections—the prime voters*—but for the mega mall list, they wanted them all.

"These voters are a gold mine," Rob said, as they sorted the voter list by street address. They even logged onto MapQuest.com and created maps to guide the walkers. "Let's get these Walking Books* over to Max right away so Mary and the volunteers can start tonight."

Linda had just come back from the printer with a handout highlighting Mary's opposition to the mall.

"These are really cool," Linda said, pointing to the door hook feature and picture of the humongous mall they lifted off the developer's website. Every one of these Mary could deliver to a mall opponent was practically a sure vote.

They looked at the results of the last two elections where the town supervisor, a Republican, won. They noticed that in four of Mary's precincts, the supervisor came out on top, but Democrats who were on the same ballot in other races such as district attorney beat out their Republican opponents.

"This means that the voters in these four precincts could go either way," Rob explained. "They've shown they'll vote Republican for supervisor and then cross over and vote Democrat for someone else. We want them to cross over to Mary, so we'll hit these areas hard."

Of the five remaining precincts, two were solid Republican and two solid Democrat. Rob printed out voter lists from the Democrat precincts. The final district, number 10, had more enrolled Democrats, but leaned Republican in the elections they analyzed. Rob printed out that list as well. For good measure, he created lists of all Democrat women in the Republican areas.

Rob spelled it out for the campaign team:

An average of 10,000 voters cast a ballot in District 3 in the last two supervisor races. This amounted to about 1,000 per precinct. Rob's projected vote tally went like this:

PRECINCT	TAG	MARY	AMATO
1	Mall	650	350
2	Swing	525	475
3	Swing	525	475
4	Swing	525	475
5	Swing	525	475
6	DEM	600	400
7	DEM	600	400
8	GOP	350	650
9	GOP	350	650
10	DEM but votes GOP	500	500
TOTAL		5150	4850

"It's a tall order counting all those swing votes," Carol said to Rob.

"I know. That's why we have to hit them hard."

Rob also pointed out another part of the campaign he was relying on: the organizations supporting Mary.

"I have the voter lists from the environmental and taxpayer groups, Friends of the Library, Rotary and a few other service clubs Max was able to get and we picked up the endorsement of the Communication

Workers union which is unhappy with the deal the town cut with the cable company. That's a thousand voters altogether. If we can get half of them to come out and vote, I think we'll be okay."

Contributing to Rob's optimism was the fact that a good majority of these voters came from the districts that were reliably Republican. He also felt good about the 500 "I'm With You, Mary" cards they entered into the data base.

They ended the meeting by going over the voter registration drive—85 new registrants so far, 75 signing up as Democrats. Rob also reported that 750 "Do Me a Favor" cards, hand addressed and signed by Mary's supporters, went out, in addition to 225 Absentee Voter letters.

CHAPTER TWELVE
THE EXCITING CONCLUSION

12

From boning up on the issues and nailing down her platform to naming her team and raising money, Mary built a solid foundation to win a seat on the Centerville Town Council. Let's sit back and watch as her campaign applies the lessons learned.

Mary was now up against incumbent Councilman Frank Amato, who was going for his third term. He was a Republican who prided himself on his conservative values and watching out for the bottom line. He's a friend of the business community and helps his contributors cut through government red tape. Mary saw him many times at meetings and although he talked a good game on economic development and creating jobs, Centerville's weak tax base and low employment rate proved otherwise. He lived at the opposite end of the district from Mary and was in favor of the mega mall.

"We can beat him," Rob told the team, reiterating his plan to build a winning majority. He summed up the strategy:

- "First, we'll make sure we get every anti-mall vote there is, so we'll hit that area really hard."

- "Next, we need to win the four swing precincts where voters have shown they could go either way."

- "Just as important, we need to focus on the two precincts where the Democrats have the edge. This is our base and I don't want to take it for granted."

- "In the precincts that usually go Republican, we'll hit the Democrats with some mail and calls, but we won't be walking there."

- "I like Precinct Ten. If we can get those Democrats off their butts, we could go even-Steven and pick up 500 votes."

- "Finally, we have some reliable blocs and lists we've put together. Getting them out to vote is the key since we already know they'll lean toward Mary."

"Let's give 'em hell," the candidate shouted.

Looking to capitalize on Mary's momentum from beating Fink and not wanting to give Amato a chance to strike first, the campaign had a mailing out the day after the primary. It took her message to all the voters in the four swing precincts and all of the Democrats and independents in the two reliably Democrat areas. They hit the Democrats in the two GOP areas and the precinct that usually goes Republican but has a large amount of enrolled Dems. Every registered voter near the mega mall site got a letter from Mary with "Stop the Mega Mall" printed on the envelope.

Rob also contacted the anti-mall leaders and organized a rally featuring Mary at the site. They prepared the following:

COUNCIL CANDIDATE MARY MORGAN OPPOSES MEGA MALL OUTLINES ECONOMIC DEVELOPMENT AND JOB CREATION PLAN

For Immediate Release………………..September 10, 2014
Contact Linda Smith…………………..……..653-555-1234

"The enormous Carson mega mall has no place in Centerville," said District 3 Council Candidate Mary Morgan today as she announced an economic development and jobs creation plan that will strengthen the town's Main Street Business District.

"We don't want Main Street to become a ghost town as this huge mall competes with shops that have been a mainstay in Centerville for more than 100 years," Morgan said. "Our economy and precious environmental resources simply cannot handle it."

Joining Morgan at an anti-mall rally was Rem Peterson, a leader in the fight against the 119-store project.

"More than 85 acres of trees and meadows would be destroyed if this monstrosity is built and a sea of asphalt would take their place," Peterson said. "Mott's River would be horribly polluted by parking lot runoff and our underground drinking water supply would be ruined."

Instead of the mega mall, Morgan proposed a scaled down mixed use of the property with affordable housing, medical offices, and parks. The development would be clustered away from Mott's River and 67 percent of the land would be undisturbed.

continued

"Morgan's plan would be an acceptable use of this land and would not lead to the destruction of our economy and environment," Peterson said.

Morgan outlined an economic revitalization package for Centerville that includes:

- Eliminating red tape so existing businesses can renovate or expand.
- Lowering taxes to allow homeowners and local businesses to thrive.
- Cutting the energy tax to make it more affordable to live and do business in Centerville.
- Renovate the Centerville Train Station and create a transportation hub to better facilitate the flow of people and commerce.

"One of the biggest roadblocks to Centerville's economic recovery is town hall," Morgan said. "Bureaucratic red tape, high taxes and fees, and the inability of our elected leaders to get our economy going is killing our tax base. They are the main reason there are no jobs."

If elected, Morgan said her top priority will be Centerville's economy and services such as parks and recreation that have fallen off with the town's poor financial health. "Our children shouldn't be playing on dirt fields because of bad management at town hall," Morgan concluded.

###

As Mary's crowd assembled at the mega mall site, another group formed across the street. It was Amato and the mall supporters. Hundreds of people showed up and the street was clogged cars.

"It looks like Woodstock," Peterson joked as he handed out fliers with bullets from Mary's press release.

Amato brought in the construction unions that would build the mall and had a large group from the Republican Party. Mary assembled her neighbors, environmentalists, and a nice contingent of supporters rounded up by Max. The two sides were evenly split.

Peterson introduced Mary and she reiterated her opposition to the mall, causing a loud cheer to rise up from her crowd.

Across the street, a man wearing a union cap yelled into a bullhorn: "No to Morgan, yes to jobs." Amato's crowd erupted and drowned out Mary. The two sides spilled into the street and started yelling at each other. The police waded in and ordered everyone to leave. Mary and Linda were glad to make it back to their car unharmed. Men in hard hats banged on the roof as they drove away.

The team reassembled at campaign headquarters.

"The press coverage is fantastic," Linda reported. "It's clear that you're against the mall and Amato's for it, but they're also talking about your economic plan. He's got nothing like that."

Rob didn't let the events of the day sidetrack the campaign. He sat with Max and focused on the phone banks and door knocking.

"Those unions will be flooding the district with callers and walkers. We need to keep up."

"Mary, your schedule is pretty heavy," Betty said to the candidate. "Are you okay with all the walking and phone calling?"

"I'm good. There are so many people helping. I'm just going along with the flow."

"Well, you're doing a great job," Rob said. "And thank you to everyone helping out. Everything's going as planned and we're really hitting on all cylinders."

Afterward, Rob sat with Carol to go over the budget. The Fundraising Coordinator was meticulous and mapped out every expense. For the mailings, she calculated postage and printing. She had the phone bill figured in and the Internet service. She covered advertising, polling, legal expenses and even had a line for food and refreshments for the volunteers.

"The way we're going, we may even have a few bucks left over," Carol said.

"Don't forget what Mary said," Rob told her. "Don't leave anything on the table. Let's blow it all."

The next day's mail contained a shocker: Amato sent out a full glossy criticizing Mary for her "negligent" voting record. It turns out that over the last 10 years, she didn't vote in the Centerville town elections three times, missed the school budget vote four times and only voted in the fire district election twice.

"If she doesn't care enough about our town to even vote, how can we count on her to serve on the Centerville Council?" Amato's mailing asked.

"I thought you didn't have anything we should worry about," Rob took Mary aside.

"I'm sorry. I just never thought of that."

"It's okay," Rob replied. "It's really petty and we going to overcome it with our next mailing."

The campaign's Researcher, Lou Rosso, pored over the town minutes since Amato took office and found he missed a couple of council meetings. Mary's mailing took him to task:

"Councilman Amato had something more important to do than vote on a measure that would provide industrial development funds to create jobs in Centerville. He missed a vote to approve the reconstruction of Mills Park and build new baseball fields for our kids. He wasn't there to vote on an environmental study for Mott's River. In fact, he failed to represent District 3 on 87 important resolutions before the town council. We deserve better than this. Vote Mary Morgan— someone you can depend on."

Rob and Linda didn't wait for Amato's next salvo. They sent out a letter from Mary challenging him to a series of debates with the League of Women's Voters, the Environmental Forum, TaxPAC, Rotary, and other groups to discuss the issues of the campaign. They knew the last thing the incumbent councilman wanted was to give his challenger publicity by sharing a stage with her. Along with the letter, they distributed a press release and drummed up the challenge in Social Media.

Mary felt great. She was out walking almost every night and wore out two pairs of shoes. Her feet hurt, but she lost 12 pounds and used it as an excuse to buy new clothes. Her fundraising picked up dramatically after she won the primary and dialing for dollars got easier. Dozens of volunteers were coming into the headquarters and Betty had them immediately list 10 people they know. Their job, if nothing else, was to make sure those 10 people voted for Mary. They also stuck around to make fundraising calls, stuff envelopes, put up signs and whatever else needed to be done.

Tom came into the headquarters one night during a campaign meeting.

"Can I talk to you, Mary?" he said, interrupting the meeting. They went into the back room.

The campaign team heard them arguing and then Tom came out in a huff.

"Is there something wrong, Tom?" Carol was the only one who knew them both well enough to speak.

"Yes, yes there is," the husband said. "This campaigning thing is going a little too far. Mary's out every night and I don't like some of the things they're saying about her."

Carol took a deep breath.

"Tom, please, sit down."

"It's just too much," said the aggravated spouse. "She doesn't come home until late at night and I hardly see her anymore. If this is how it's going to be if she gets elected, I'd rather she just lose the thing."

"Tom, what Mary is doing is very important," Carol tried to calm him. "It's very important to her and it's very important to our town. She's doing something few people have the courage to do and I think I speak for everyone here when I say we hope you have a little more patience and understanding."

"But what about..."

Carol cut him off. "Tom, we need you—Mary needs you. I know you're upset, but this thing isn't going to work without you. Mary is doing something extraordinary and she needs your help. She needs you by her side."

"What am I like the First Husband?"

"Exactly," Rob said. "It's a sacrifice doing what you and Mary are doing. It's a sacrifice for something that's very, very important."

Mary spoke next. "Tom, I know I've been neglecting you, but the campaign will be over soon and I'll go back to a more normal schedule. I promise." She gave him a hug.

I'm sorry honey," he whispered. "It's just that I missed you and was a little jealous of all these people taking your time."

"That's okay," Mary said. "Now grab a phone and let's get back to work."

The next few mailings from the candidates were on the positive side and didn't include any zingers. Mary keyed in on her business experience and hammered home her economic platform. Amato bragged about his experience on the town council and some of his economic development and job creation initiatives. They both listed the various organizations and dignitaries that support them and neither mentioned the mega mall.

With a month to go, Mary dropped her bomb.

"It's been two weeks since Mary Morgan challenged Councilman Frank Amato to debate the issues important to Centerville. His response—Nothing! What's Amato trying to hide?"

The League of Women Voter's weighed in with a letter to the editor in the Centerville Post: "Morgan is willing, now Amato has to step up to the plate and debate his vision for Centerville," the letter concluded.

The Sign Patrol built a dozen of the following:

> # IT'S BEEN **14** DAYS SINCE AMATO WON'T DEBATE MORGAN.
> # WHAT'S HE TRYING TO HIDE?

They put the signs up on main roads in front of businesses and the homes of residents that support Mary. Everyday a volunteer changed the number of days.

"People take notice," Rob explained, "They will look to see if the number changes."

Bernard had fun with it on the Internet with a digital counter that advanced every day Amato didn't debate. Mary's fans got on board and "What's He Trying to Hide?" became a rallying call.

In the meantime, Amato tried one of the oldest tricks in the book. Mary was visited by a detective investigating a break in at her opponent's campaign headquarters. Nothing was taken, just some papers knocked off desks and file cabinets opened. Amato insinuated Mary's campaign had something to do with it and for good measure produced some pictures of a few speed limit signs in town plastered with Mary's bumper stickers. He accused her campaign of being "desperate." The Post ran a tongue-in-cheek story on it that made Amato look silly. Bernard lit him up in Social Media.

Rob and Max put together an aggressive absentee voter effort. They got the list of those requesting ballots from the board of elections ahead of time and sent a letter from Mary praising them for making sure their voice is heard. Voters with military addresses received a note from Michael's friend, a wounded Desert Storm veteran, putting in a good word for Mary. The day the actual ballots were mailed out, the campaign wrote to them again.

Rob took it a step further by sending volunteers to nursing homes, long-term care facilities, and senior centers with ballot request forms. They returned when the ballots were mailed out to offer "assistance" to those making their picks.

On day 20 of Amato's refusal to debate, a call came into the headquarters. It was Amato's camp. "Enough already. Let's do it."

Mary's team pounced: "Amato Finally Does the Right Thing—Agrees to Debate Morgan," Linda's headline rang. Bernard promoted it online like an armistice had been signed ending the Great War and the two sides were going to meet at Potsdam.

"We're going to need a bigger auditorium," Rob figured.

Amato's initial refusal to debate Mary made the issue much bigger than it had to be and focused public attention on the race. Her strategy put the incumbent in the hot seat and capitalized on the publicity. Now, Mary had to hold her own as she faced off with the incumbent.

Real Life Scenario: Mitt Romney's first debate with President Obama was a turning point in the campaign. The president seemed flat and unprepared. He didn't look like he wanted to be there. The challenger's poll results jumped and the Obama team went into hiding to prepare for the next one. They had Obama practice against a Romney stand-in and made sure all the president's answers were well-rehearsed. The difference in the two debates was dramatic and Romney could not score the knockout his side had hoped.

Mary was nervous going in, but Rob reminded her that great confidence will spring from her thorough preparation. Indeed, the team went above and beyond getting Mary ready and practicing with Lou Rosso standing in as Amato was a big help. There wasn't much that was going to come up, they thought, that Mary hadn't rehearsed.

Mary peaked out from behind the curtain and saw the crowd. She took a deep breath and was energized. Amato looked fidgety and nervous.

The debate was sponsored by the League of Women Voters and its Centerville Chapter president, Karen Williams, was the moderator. Each candidate was allowed a two-minute introduction and then one minute to answer the questions posed by the moderator. After every response, the other side was allotted a minute to comment on what their opponent said. Afterward, three members of the audience would pose a question to each candidate.

Though she was a little jittery, Mary did fine. Rob was pleased that she stuck to the script and had interjected a little humor in the proceedings. She incorporated anecdotes and personal stories into her answers. Both camps obviously concluded that attacking each other wouldn't be helpful, though Mary got some digs in about Amato's economic ideas being similar to hers and Amato harped on his experience vs. Mary's lack thereof.

Rob was impressed—and so was the audience—when Mary stood up during the Q&A and dipped into crowd. Up to that point the two candidates sat in the front of the room at a small table, isolated from the people. The fact that Mary got up and went to them had a powerful affect.

And then a gift from heaven: When answering a question about what programs he would cut to bring spending down, Amato replied, "I don't know why everyone is so worried about cutting programs. If we need more money, we can always raise taxes."

Mary's eyes almost popped out of her head.

"Mr. Amato has summed up exactly what's wrong at town hall," she told the audience with gusto. "Raising taxes is not the answer. Sharpening our pencils and working harder is what we need to do to make our town more affordable without cutting needed programs. For me, taking more and more money from the taxpayers is never an option."

Mary's team swung into action. Bernard had been videotaping the event and a clip of Amato's blunder with Mary's response flew out at the speed of light. As people were still milling around, they did a clip with Mary expanding on her anti-tax position and pulled in a few people who thought raising taxes was a terrible idea. Rob rewrote Mary's next mailing to highlight Amato's tax flub and Linda issued a press release calling on Amato to retract his statement.

Amato tried to explain he "chose his words poorly" and even pledged not to raise taxes, but the damage was done. He refused additional debates leaving Mary's campaign to conclude: "Now we know what he was trying to hide."

Five days after the debate the pollster conducted the final tracking poll. Mary had the edge over Amato head-to-head by three percentage points. With a margin of error at five points, the election could go either way. Her numbers skyrocketed with woman voters and went down a little with men. Younger people were starting to come around, but her support from seniors dropped even though Amato said he would raise taxes. Voters believed that both candidates were strong on economic issues and Mary's numbers around the mega mall went up dramatically.

Rob adjusted the mailings accordingly. He doubled down with women voters and young people by mailing to not only Democrats and independents, but Republicans as well. He did a special mailing to all seniors highlighting Amato's blunder and keying in on the need for cutting taxes and making Centerville more affordable. He also reminded the people living near the mega mall that Mary was dead set against it.

Amato's mailings came fast and furious. He hit Mary on her lack of government experience and said she would be an "economic disaster." The rumor was that the Republican Party was spending a lot of money but didn't have too many people on the streets.

"Amato's camp is getting the same poll results we are," Rob said. "He's gotta go negative to bring Mary's numbers down. He's going after men on job issues and is telling seniors she's going to tax them out of their homes. He's trying, but I don't think he's got any credibility with the young people because they don't read his mail and are only getting their information from the Internet, where he's weak."

"Great," Mary said. "Keep up the good work."

Linda came running in with a Media Advisory hot off the printer.

"Amato's having a press conference," she said waiving the paper. "Subject: Jobs and a surprise endorsement."

"I'll go check it out," Lou said.

"I'll go with you," said Rob.

Amato assembled about 20 people in front of the vacant Carr store on Main Street. He released an economic plan almost identical to Mary's and said her "anti-business stance would cost Centerville jobs and cause taxes to go up." According to Amato, "Mary Morgan would be a disaster for not only Centerville's working families, but seniors and young people as well."

"Guess who the surprise endorsement was from?" Lou asked the team when he returned. "Kingsley! That big rat was at his side and you know who else was there? Bratton."

"He was in their camp all along. No wonder he was so eager to help," Rob said, putting his fingers up like quotation marks when he said the word, help.

He called a meeting of the Rapid Response Team. Amato's press conference appeared in the Centerville Post's online edition and the team sent out an email to a select list of Mary's supporters they could trust with instructions to go on the Post's site and comment. They encouraged them to follow the theme of this statement from Mary's campaign:

Councilman Amato's press conference shows just how far a politician will go to mislead the public in order to get elected. His economic plan is almost identical to Mary Morgan's except for one key fact: He's been a councilman for five years and hasn't done anything mentioned in his plan to get Centerville's economy back on track. Mary Morgan has owned and operated a business in Centerville for over 25 years. Unlike Amato, she's created jobs and knows how to balance a budget. Mary Morgan is the Democrat candidate for District 3, regardless of the deal Amato made with the Democrat boss to appear at his press conference. It would be better for Centerville's taxpayers—working families, senior citizens and young people alike—if these two spent less time on politics and more time on the getting our economy back in order.—Rob Carter, Campaign Manager

Linda had the statement over to the Centerville Post in time for the next morning's paper and the Rapid Response Team, with help from Bernard, got Rob's rebuttal everywhere on the Internet. They got another pleasant surprise when a Post editorial called out Amato and Kingsley's cozy relationship with the mega mall developers and ran a ringing endorsement for Mary.

Linda made a flyer with the Post's endorsement on one side and a list of the groups and organizations supporting her on the other.

"The Democrats are pissed," Lou reported at the campaign meeting. "They don't like their leader sidling up to the Republicans and want to come out in a big way for Mary."

"Let's do a rally," Rob jumped up. "After all, Mary's the candidate of the Democratic Party, despite the deals its leader is cutting on the side."

"What are the other council candidates thinking?" Mary asked.

"Let's invite them and see what they do," Rob replied.

The campaign rallied at town hall on the Saturday before the vote. Max and the rest of the staff went into overdrive calling Democratic committee members and voters who said they were leaning toward Mary. Rob set up a PA system to make sure Mary would be heard loud and clear. About 200 people showed up, including the Democrat candidate for supervisor and two council challengers. They took the mic one by one with each reiterating the importance of having the Democrat team at town hall to implement their economic plan and provide better services to the residents.

Also in the audience were representatives of the various groups supporting Mary and her running mates.

"We will make history," Mary said to the exuberant throng. "When we win on Tuesday, the Democrats will take control of our town for the first time in 50 years."

The crowd went wild.

"There's nothing left to do now but get out the vote," Rob said as the rally wrapped up. He made sure Mary pressed the flesh with each and every person there and Max followed up by giving them his card and getting their contact information.

Mary's team planned an aggressive GOTV effort and the first order of business on Election Day was to make sure the people who said they support Mary actually got out to vote. As they did in the primary, poll watchers reported back to headquarters on who on their list didn't yet vote and those people were dragged out. The phone banks were humming.

"My fingers are crossed," Mary showed the team, uncrossing them to dial another number. Even Tom took the day off to call his list to make sure they vote. Linda took Mary's picture at the voting booth and posted it as a reminder for everyone to hit the polls. Suffice it to say, there wasn't a person connected to Mary through the Internet who wasn't reminded to vote thanks to a steady diet of posts, emails and tweets.

At six o'clock Rob reported that voter turnout was high, especially among the Democrats. "That's a good sign," he said. "We're turning out our side."

At quarter to nine, people started coming into the headquarters to wait for the results. Rob set up a laptop computer and projector to show the precinct totals on the wall for everyone to see.

At 9:10, the first precinct reported, a Republican area. Advantage, Amato—55%-45%. The crowd gasped.

Next was a swing area, neck and neck.

"Don't worry, your areas didn't come in yet," Rob whispered to Mary. "Plus we haven't heard from the mega mall voters."

The results refreshed: Amato 53%, Mary 47%. A groan went out from the crowd.

"No worries," Rob responded. "That's Amato's other area coming in. Just wait."

The next refresh showed it 51% Mary, 49% Amato— a swing precinct came in for Mary.

The crowd cheered and Tom gave his wife a hug.

The screen blinked: 50-50, it was a dead heat.

Everyone held their breath. Then the mega mall area reported, 52-48 Mary.

The crowd swooned.

At 9:30, the final precincts were in. Mary was down by 62 votes.

The crowd gulped as Mary looked on stoically.

Rob jumped up on a chair.

"Ladies and gentlemen please! It's not over! They still have to count the absentee ballots."

The crowd erupted: "Mary! Mary! Mary!"

The attorney, Marvin Adler, went into the back to make a phone call. He got the commissioner of the Centerville Board of Elections on the line and formally requested that all ballots be secured for a recount. He also confirmed that the absentee ballots were locked away and would be opened in the morning. He and Lou sped down to the BOE headquarters where they encountered a team from the Republicans. Lou would join a representative of the other side and a BOE staffer to babysit the ballots overnight.

There were 262 absentee ballots cast and at eight the next morning, the BOE staff opened them one at a time as the two teams looked on.

"Step back, give them room," an officious-looking gentleman yelled.

Each side tallied the vote in concert with the official score keeper who handled each ballot like it was an original copy of the Declaration of Independence.

Rob showed up and reminded everyone within earshot that two of Mary's running mates won big as did the Republican supervisor and one of his running mates.

"Control of the town council is hanging on this race," he said to no one in particular. There was no need to scrutinize the absentee ballots in the other races.

The check marks in Mary's column grew and grew and she overcame Amato's 62 vote lead with 50 ballots left to count.

"If it keeps going our way, we win," Rob said, hardly hiding his enthusiasm.

"Done," the BOE official announced. "Mary Morgan wins District Three by 17 votes."

"Wait," one of the Republicans shouted. "What about the ballots? We demand a recount of all the ballots."

The group went into an adjoining room where the voter cards sat in tall piles. The BOE boss spoke: "We are going to run them through a special optical reader one at a time. You are free to observe the process and we will give you the final count immediately upon completion."

At the end of the day, the elections board announced it had adjusted Mary's margin of victory down from 17 to 12 votes on account of five cards being unreadable. She was still the winner.

Amato's side immediately filed a court brief to challenge the results. Adler assembled a legal team of attorneys and investigators and they argued with Amato's folks over every name, address and marking on each of the 262 absentee ballots. Amato's side even visited many of the voters to confirm if they indeed filled out the ballot. Many were older residents who were afraid to sign an affidavit swearing to their vote.

After two weeks of deliberation, the court agreed with Amato's arguments that 16 of Mary's absentee votes were invalid and readjusted the vote tally to show him winning by a grand total of four votes.

Mary's team was crushed and her husband, Tom, urged her to give it up so they could get back to their normal lives.

"We've taken it this far," Mary said to her team. "Tell Marvin to appeal."

"It's three thousand dollars," Tom put his foot down. "Now we're throwing good money after bad. Where the hell are we going to get three thousand dollars?"

"He's right in one respect," Rob told Carol on the side. "We're completely tapped out."

"Get Adler on the phone," Carol ordered. "How confident are you we can win the appeal?" she asked him.

"Pretty sure," he answered. "The lower court missed a few key points. I think the appellate will overrule them."

"Marvin, we love you, but we're broke. You've done a great job and we really appreciate it," Carol said. "How about this: take us all the way and if we win, Mary can raise money to pay the fee pretty easily as councilwoman. If we lose, it's pro bono."

Adler didn't hesitate. "Done! I'll get the appeal ready."

Adler faced off with lawyers he'd never seen before, experts brought in by the state Republicans. They fussed over ballots and addresses with Adler's thrust being that the people voted how they voted and no legal arguments can change that.

The panel of five judges split their decision with three upholding the lower court and two against. Mary was still on the losing side as they headed to the state's highest court.

"Just like in the primary battle," Marvin said, "the higher court should go with the people's right to have their vote count."

Since Amato was already a councilman, he went on with business as usual and made it a point to trump up his economic plans. He even introduced a resolution waiving a part of the environmental review process to expedite the mega mall. The neighborhood was livid.

The appellate judges were on their own schedule and the days dragged on. Mary was paralyzed and could hardly tend to her business. Tom wouldn't even talk to her.

And then one chilly afternoon Mary's cell phone screen flashed "Adler."

"Marvin, what? Tell me some good news," Mary could hardly contain herself.

"Congratulations, Madam Councilwoman. The judges saw it our way. It's over. You got your twelve votes back."

Mary texted the team and they assembled at the HQ for an impromptu victory party which Rob turned into a "postmortem" to discuss what went right and what went wrong with the campaign. Mary told Rob to go first.

According to the Campaign Manager, Carol's fundraising program and Mary's willingness to dial for dollars made all the difference in the world in taking out the entrenched incumbent.

"Although we didn't match him dollar for dollar, we had enough to make it competitive," Rob declared.

The money allowed Mary to keep up with her opponent in mailings and advertising and she stayed consistent with her message of economic growth and creating jobs. When her polls revealed how she was doing, she responded by doubling up on mailings to women and young people and reiterated her message to senior citizens on taxes and affordability. She aggressively pursued the anti-mega mall vote and added the issue of revitalizing parks and recreation facilities to appeal to women with families.

Mary's campaign rallies—at the mega mall site and with the Democrats—nailed down her base and her GOTV program made sure her people voted.

Bernard made the dinosaur incumbent pay for his weak Internet and Social Media presence and bolstered Mary's coffers by making it easy for people to donate online. He amassed a large email data base of both donors and voters and found Mary many new friends who normally wouldn't have any interest in a town election.

Working with Rob, Linda kept the press releases, statements, updates, and other campaign material coming. Her relationship with the editor of the Centerville Post helped swing the coverage in Mary's favor, and it didn't hurt that they took out a few back page ads. The Rapid Response Team insured that Amato's attacks were challenged at every turn and, in fact, not much appeared on the Internet that didn't promote Mary's side of the story.

Another huge factor in Mary's win was Max Baumgartner and his ability to recruit and manage the troops. Mary had a built-in base from the Rotary Club which made up for the Democrat insiders who supported her primary opponent, Fink, and were miffed she was on the ballot instead of him. It didn't hurt Mary's efforts when Kingsley showed his true colors and jumped over to the other side, a move Mary swiftly counteracted through her Democrat rally with the other candidates.

The team did well in recruiting volunteers and then making sure they got people to vote. A vast network formed with people contacting people. Without the person-to-person GOTV strategy on Election Day, Mary would not have won by 12 votes.

Of course, Marvin Adler and his team saved the day by beating back—albeit at the highest court—the other side's legal challenges.

Mary got a taste of campaign treachery when Henry Bratton tried to derail her campaign with bad advice and Amato stealing her economic plan. She also felt the impact of organized labor when they crashed her mega mall rally and hit the streets to work against her.

To counter that, she courted the environmental and taxpayer groups, but was careful not to be anti-development when it came to the economy and creating jobs. Her mega mall press release went out of its way to talk about economic development and job creation to appeal to the people not living near the mall. Amato tried to tarnish Mary on her voting record, but the campaign countered it pretty well by revealing his missed votes on the town council.

It turned out that many town employees voted for Mary, partly because she didn't drag them into her criticisms about town hall and also because of Amato's imperious attitude that looked down on the average worker. It will be easier for Mary to get things done through the town employees than it was for Amato.

Mary's Researcher proved valuable by unearthing material on her opponents that could be used in the campaign. Her debate challenge had great traction and she held her own by being practiced and prepared when they finally went head to head. Amato's gift from heaven about raising taxes played nicely into Mary's hand.

All and all, Mary ran a professional, well-managed campaign that was constantly fine-tuned through all stages of its planning and execution.

Amato's campaign, on the other hand, suffered from the ills of an incumbent backed by a long-standing political party. Instead of recruiting supporters and energizing them to get out the vote, Amato's race had a "stay away" feel to it. The political bosses didn't want a lot of people involved because that would mean more mouths to feed, more people asking for favors. Plus, new blood would be a threat to the existing power structure. So they played it close to the vest, spending money freely, but failing to harness the power of people.

Mary had waited months to hit Rob with her favorite line uttered by Robert Redford in the movie, "The Candidate," after he won a longshot bid for the U.S. Senate.

"Hey Rob," she smiled, "What do we do now?"

CHAPTER THIRTEEN

CAMPAIGN OVERVIEW

13

Here's an overview of a winning campaign:

Create your Narrative, Platform, and Elevator Speech covering who you are and what you will do for the voters; set it in stone and don't waiver. Practice until you can recite them in your sleep. You can make minor adjustments along the way, but don't flip flop. This will confuse the voters and make you look like the type of politician they hate.

Your persona and approach to the issues will be the primary reasons that people contribute money, volunteer their time, and vote for you. They want to be invested in you and what you stand for. Put up a professional image and fine tune your public speaking skills.

Write key points, anecdotes, jokes quips, stories, etc. on note cards; create new cards for different situations, events, meetings. Remember the Great Admonition, *Never say anything you haven't thought about beforehand,* and don't forget the mic is always on.

Show people you have what it takes to win by running a credible fundraising operation; create a budget and goals. Meticulously plan your events and other fundraising activities. Put a huge emphasis on money and raise as much as you can. Make sure your efforts are well managed and impressive, including what your people are saying to your potential donors. Don't be afraid to ask for money.

Find out the legalities of running for office. How do you get on the ballot? What are the deadlines? Make your candidacy bullet proof so you don't get knocked off on a technicality.

Seek learned advice and line up an attorney with election experience to watch your back every step of the way. Be open to criticism and always be willing to improve.

Build a solid campaign team and fill all the critical roles. Your Campaign Manager and Fundraiser are vital, so choose them well. Spend as much time with them as necessary to create a detailed game plan. Let your team execute the plan; stay out of their way.

Announce your candidacy; be humble and grateful.

Use a calendar to plot everything that needs to be done; set deadlines and conduct regular meetings with the staff. Work from the calendar and a meeting agenda/check list to make sure everybody is doing what they're supposed to.

Schedule all of your activities: dialing for dollars, knocking on doors, meetings, debates, etc. Figure in some downtime so you don't wear yourself to a frazzle. Get a good Driver or two and always have people with you in public.

Have a long talk with your significant others, make sure they're an asset and don't drag you down.

Set up a headquarters, make sure it's properly equipped and stocked with beverages and food.

Find out what's on the minds of the electorate; don't take it for granted that you know what they're thinking. Conduct formal and informal polls. Set up Google Alerts.

Go to meetings of the office you are seeking, attend related meetings; farm for issues, supporters, voters.

Once your system is working, don't micromanage. You are the candidate, so go out and campaign. Your team will tell you exactly where you need to be and what to do.

Don't be paralyzed by inaction or waiting for someone else; set your plan and do it.

Break down where your votes will come from and tailor your activities to drawing them out; create lists of potential voters, build a winning majority.

Build a data base of volunteers, supporters, donors, organizations, and voters; add to it for the rest of your political life.

Seek out political parties, groups, clubs, organizations, blocs, etc. and earn their support. If it's a partisan race, get on your party's ticket; find out exactly what they're willing to do for you and help them do it.

Touch base with your running mates; coordinate your efforts.

Beware of spies, chiselers, double-dealers and people who want to spend your money; don't let anyone disrupt your carefully laid plans or drive away your supporters.

Have your team agree on the methods you will use to connect with the voters:

- Face-to-face: Meetings, events, door-to-door, debates
- Phone: Phone banks, robo calls
- Mail: Letters, flats, cards; postage, labels; choose designer, printer, mail house

- Advertising: TV, radio, newspaper, billboards, Google, Social Media
- Internet: Website, Social Media, email
- Media: Press releases/conferences, letters to editor, press kits, editorial interviews, endorsements

How you incorporate these methods into your campaign will be dictated by your budget. As early as possible, figure out what everything will cost and fine tune your strategy from there. Use the calendar to plan every detail: when will the mailing come back from the designer, go to the printer, drop at the post office?

Double down on the tactics that don't require a lot of money: face-to-face campaigning, phoning, media relations and the Internet, particularly email and Social Media. Pump out a steady stream of material; put your stuff in front of the voters: press releases, posts, videos, pictures, commentary, position papers, white papers, letters to the editor, speeches, tweets, updates, announcements; feed the Internet and Social Media.

Get photographed and taped. Fact check your writing, fix typos, read it out loud

Aggressively recruit volunteers and make it clear what you want them to do; keep them busy. Don't forget to thank them, feed them, and cheer them on. Emphasize "I'm With You" and "Do Me a Favor" cards.

Organize press conferences, rallies, meetings.

Seek out endorsements; get on the good side of influencers, VIP's, reporters, editors, running mates; provide them with brochures and professional press kits.

Keep an eye on your opponent and adjust your campaign accordingly. If they attack, how will you respond? Are you going to attack them? Create a Rapid Response Team.

Don't leave it up to fate that people will actually vote. Create an aggressive GOTV plan and don't forget the absentee voters and new registrants. Make sure you vote.

Invite your supporters to your HQ to hear the election results; thank them. Win/lose with dignity, don't gloat/whine; set yourself up for the next step.

CHAPTER FOURTEEN
CAMPAIGN CHECKLIST

14

Use this checklist to make sure you leave no stones unturned in your march to victory.

☐ Commit to run; notify family, friends, potential supporters.

☐ Reach an understanding with your significant others.

☐ Take stock of strengths/weaknesses—polish your image.

☐ Attend meetings of the office you seek; related meetings.

☐ Gather information about your seat and the issues; talk to people.

☐ Campaign Team:

    __Campaign Manager
    __Treasurer
    __Fundraising Coordinator
    __Secretary/Scheduler
    __Office Manager
    __Spokesperson/Publicist
    __Website/Social Media Manager
    __Volunteer Coordinator/Recruiter
    __Attorney

    ___Researcher
    ___Driver
    ___Sign Patrol
    ___Pollster
    ___Consultant

☐ Team meeting.

☐ Announce candidacy.

☐ Legal requirements: get on ballot, money issues.

☐ Campaign calendar; meeting agenda.

☐ Formal/informal polls; clarify issues, how you will address them.

☐ Write/practice Narrative, Elevator Speech, Platform Speech; memorize 10 points.

☐ Fundraising:

    ___Dial for Dollars
    ___Direct Mail
    ___Fundraising Events
    ___Email
    ___Online Donations

☐ Recruit volunteers.

☐ Rapid Response Team.

☐ Budget, bank account, checks.

☐ Graphics package for letterhead, online image; photographs.

☐ Online Platform—Website, Facebook, Twitter, LinkedIn, YouTube, Instagram, etc.

☐ Email data bases: donors and voters; update often.

☐ Email service (Constant Contact, Mail Chimp, Campaigner, Elite Mail).

☐ Announcement press conference, press release.

☐ Set up headquarters.

☐ Office equipment: phones, answering machine, computers, projector, printers, copy machines, scanners, Internet, fax, desks, chairs, easels, etc.

☐ Staples: pens, pencils, press kit folders, markers, highlighters, paper clips, tape, rubber bands, erasers, paper products, writing pads, post–its, message pads, filing, CDs, thumb drives, white out, envelopes, copy machine/printer paper, ink, toner, calendar, staplers/staples, glue sticks, pushpins, thumbtacks, paper towels, napkins, plates, cups, plastic wear, toilet paper, soap, cleaners, décor, etc.

☐ HQ food and beverages.

☐ Voter lists; build winning majority.

☐ Supporting organizations, endorsements.

☐ Create voter contact game plan; start campaigning.

> ___Face-to-face: Meetings, events, door-to-door, debates
> ___Phone: Phone banks, robo calls
> ___Mail: Letters, flats, cards; postage, labels; choose designer, printer, mail house
> ___Advertising: TV, radio, newspaper, billboards, Google, Social Media
> ___Internet: Website, Social Media, email
> ___Media: Press releases/conferences, letters to editor, press kits, editorial interviews, endorsements

☐ Palm card/brochure, Do Me a Favor and I'm With You cards.

☐ Giveaways: bags, balloons, bookmarks, bumper stickers, buttons, clips, combs, door hangers, golf tees, jar openers, key chains, letter openers, magnets, nail files, pads, pencils, pens, posters, pot holders, rulers, stickers, yard signs.

☐ Advertising plan: newspapers, radio, TV, billboards, Internet.

☐ Direct mail plan: designer, printer, voter lists, labeling, postage.

☐ Volunteer activities; scripts for phone, walking, fundraising, voter ID, GOTV.

☐ Sign Patrol.

☐ Press releases, posts, videos, pictures, commentary, position papers, white papers, letters to the editor, speeches, tweets, updates, announcements.

☐ Initiatives:

    __Announce a new idea
    __Respond to a current event
    __Highlight a new aspect of your campaign
    __Trot out a major endorsement
    __Criticize your opponent
    __Answer criticism
    __Help someone with a cause
    __Release statistics
    __Report a victory
    __Disclose legal action

☐ Monitor opponents, media, Internet; set up Google Alerts.

☐ Brainstorm; schedule press conferences.

☐ Voter Registration Drive.

☐ Absentee Ballot Program.

☐ Get Out The Vote.

☐ Election night victory party.

GLOSSARY

Absentee Voter: People who can't make it to the polls on Election Day and cast their vote through an absentee ballot. These include people who will be out of town, hospital and nursing home patients, and the military.

Base: A group of people naturally expected to vote for you.

Bid: A campaign for an elected office.

Big Mo: The momentum gained by a candidate after a victory.

Blanks: Voters not registered under a particular political party; also referred to as independents.

Bloc: A voter group tied to a specific issue or cause.

Blue State: A state controlled by Democrats, particularly in a presidential election.

Carpet Bagger: A person who moves to an area for the purpose of running for office.

Constituency: A group of people that elects representatives.

Dialing for Dollars: Calling people on the phone for a contribution.

Earned Media: Free news coverage generated by press releases, news conferences, and other campaign activities.

Election Bug: An obsessive mental condition that drives people to run for elective office.

Electorate: The people who are entitled to vote in an election (not to be confused with registrants—those who have actually signed up to vote—or voters—those who actually vote).

Favorables: Poll responses that are in your favor.

Freedom of Information Law: Most government entities must, by law, provide taxpayers with public information if a FOIL request is submitted.

Frontrunner: The candidate favored to win.

General Election: A regular election of candidates for office.

Gerrymandering: Drawing election district boundaries to give certain people or parties an advantage.

Glad Handing: The art of shaking hands and making contact with voters.

Incumbent: The person currently holding an elected office.

Mail Merge: A Computer program that inserts names, addresses, and other data into letters, advertisements, and other materials to maximize their impact.

Mail House: A company that handles large mailing jobs.

Mandate: The authority given by the voters to an elected official to carry out a policy or course of action.

Media Advisory: A statement letting the press know about press conferences and other activities.

Name Recognition: The term for people being able to recognize and/or know something about you.

Nepotism: Political favoritism based on family connections

Nod: An organization's endorsement of a candidate.

Off Year: Since candidates for the U.S. Congress are elected every two years, the year they are not running is referred to as an off year. May also refer to one of the three years when there isn't a presidential election and the years when state offices aren't up.

Party Faithful: Active supporters of a political organization.

Patronage: Jobs and favors given on the basis of politics.

Perennial Candidate: People who frequently express interest in running for office, but never get elected.

Plank: Set of issues or beliefs a candidate stands for.

Plurality: The number of votes received by a winning candidate above the amount received by the losers; the winning margin.

Political Action Committee (PAC): An organization that raises money to support candidates or a cause.

Politician: A person in politics as a profession; an office holder.

Politico: An informal term for politician.

Press Release: A statement on something you want to media to cover.

Primary Election: A vote to determine the choice of a political party to run in a General Election.

Prime Voter: Registrants who can be relied on to vote such as those who cast ballots in the last few general elections and primaries.

Red State: A state controlled by Republicans, particularly in a presidential election.

Safe Seat: An elected office considered to be easily won by a particular party or person.

Soccer Moms: Groups of women voters focused on family issues.

Spoiler: A candidate with views similar to another who takes votes from that candidate causing another candidate to win.

Stakeholders: People who have donated to a campaign or are otherwise invested in the outcome.

Swing Voter: A person who doesn't normally vote by party line who can swing an election either way.

Ticket Splitter: A person who votes for candidates from different parties.

Walking Books: Packages including maps and the names and addresses of targeted voters used for door knocking.

APPENDIX

Mary's Budget

Direct mail (design, printing, labels, postage):	7,000
Advertising (radio, newspaper, billboards):	4,500
Legal services (Adler, partners, investigators):	4,000
Pollster:	2,500
Campaign Manager:	2,500
Website/Social Media Manager:	2,000
Campaign HQ rental:	1,500
Equipment rental (printers, computers, phones):	990
Food/beverages:	880
Phone/Internet:	825
Palm cards:	750
Utilities:	645
Cell phones:	625
Handouts (pads, pens, combs, nail files):	600
Yard signs:	525
Gas:	525
Bumper stickers:	500
Office supplies (post card stock, CDs, folders, etc.):	475
Stamps:	445
Lunch/dinners:	425
Door hangers:	325
Robo calls:	250
BOE/website fees:	125

Total $32,910

Real Life Scenario: Thanks in no small part to the talents and hard work of her fundraiser, Carol, and Mary's willingness to call people and ask them for money, the campaign team hit their goal of $30,000, including the thousand dollars in seed money put in by the candidate. This left $2,910 owed to Marvin Adler. Mary was sworn into office January 1 and held her first fundraiser as an elected official later that month. She raised enough money to pay off Marvin and her own $1,000, with $9,300 left over to build for her reelection (or maybe she'll run for something else—stay tuned!)

MARY MORGAN FOR CENTERVILLE TOWN COUNCIL

I'M WITH YOU, MARY!

Name:_____

Address:_____

Phone:_____

Email:_____

X Yes, I'd like to help with Mary's campaign.

Election Day: November 4

PLEASE DO ME A FAVOR

Dear *Paul*

My friend Mary Morgan is running for Centerville Town Council and I would greatly appreciate it if you vote for her on November 4. Mary stands for lower taxes and better services from town hall. Your vote counts, so please make sure you get to the polls between 9 a.m. to 9 p.m. Thank you very much.

Sincerely,

Joe McDowell

About the Author:

Robert Chartuk is a 30-year veteran of election campaigns at the local, state, and federal levels. A former newspaper reporter, he was counted on to "write the thing"—the strategy, press release, white paper, speech. "A lot of power is vested in the person who gets the ball rolling," Chartuk explains, and he was in the driver's seat for many successful elections. Here, for the first time, are his decades of experience, Real Life Scenarios, and tips and techniques taken right from the campaign trail. There's no political mumbo jumbo here or academic discussion, just real life advice on how to win an election. If you are running for office or involved in a campaign and you want to win, Chartuk will get you there, one vote at a time.

www.ingramcontent.com/pod-product-compliance
Lightning Source LLC
Chambersburg PA
CBHW060333290526
45793CB00003B/611